Crafts
Through the Year

Crafts
Through the Year

How to make traditional gifts and decorations for every season

Thomas and Petra Berger

Floris
Books

Translated by Polly Lawson

Photographs by Wim Steenkamp, Thomas Berger and Frits Dijkhof
Illustrations by Ronald Heuninck
Transparencies by Petra Berger, Aeola Baan and Sigrid Brandligt

First published in Dutch as *Seizoenenknutselboek*
by Uitgeverij Christofoor, Zeist in 2000
First published in its current form by Floris Books, Edinburgh in 2000
This edition published in 2011
Fourth printing 2021

British Library CIP Data available
ISBN 978-086315-828-5
Printed in Poland through Hussar

MIX
Paper from
responsible sources
FSC® C144789
FSC
www.fsc.org

Floris Books supports sustainable forest management
by printing this book on materials made from wood that
comes from responsible sources and reclaimed material

Contents

Foreword

This book has been put together from parts of our earlier three books, *The Christmas Craft Book*, *The Easter Craft Book* and *The Harvest Craft Book*. We now have a book with over 150 crafts through the year.

The seasons gradually follow each other in the eternal cycle of nature through the year. Many of the ideas here help to bring what is happening outside in nature indoors as crafts that can be made at home. After the long darkness of the winter months the buds on trees and bushes begin to swell. In her picture book *The Story of the Root Children*, Sibylle von Olfers tells us how the root children wake from their sleep with Mother Earth and come up from the earth as flower children, and we describe how to make your own Mother Earth and flower children figures. Nature clothes herself in green leaves and a dazzling array of colourful blossoms, which we explain how to press and dry. Depending on the warmth of the sun, the harvest begins in late summer. Harvest time offers a wealth of colourful material for craft activities.

As well as the development of the natural year we follow the cycle of Christian festivals. Nature begins to show life at Easter time, the festival of life overcoming death. It is a festival which dates from long before the coming of Christianity. The crucifixion and resurrection are much too difficult for little children to grasp, but they can make and play with symbols of new life in nature: of eggs, chicks, lambs and Easter rabbits and hares.

As spring merges into early summer, Christianity celebrates the festivals of Ascension and Whitsun. Both festivals are related to the sky and the air and the way living creatures open themselves to them. Symbols of this season are winged creatures (birds and butterflies) and the unfolding of flowers.

In summer, June 24 is the festival of St John, a time to live outdoors amidst nature. It is a time for going out and gathering material (take a bag with you on every outing). Don't wait for autumn storms — many things are lying on the ground, without any need to plunder your garden or local park.

Ancient accounts and legends tell how the Archangel Michael was appointed by God to undertake the battle with the dragon. He is not only the vanquisher of the dragon; he is also depicted as weighing souls — the one who stands at the gate of heaven weighing the harvest of a human life. His festival is on September 29.

Halloween has its origin in the Celtic festival of Samhain, which celebrated the first day of winter on November 1. The spirits of the dead and other supernatural creatures — fairies, witches and goblins — were about on that night. Turnip and pumpkin lanterns are made to symbolise the last afterthought of the summer's ripening strength.

Of all the festivals in the course of the Christian year Christmas has a special place. This is the festival of the light that came to earth, the festival of the birth of the child Jesus. This is the festival which we celebrate afresh each year, which requires so much preparation, especially with children in the family. It is a challenge to make it peaceful amid all the rush. It is best to begin your inner preparation for Christmas at the end of November or the beginning of December; that is, at the beginning of Advent, for Advent is the time of expectation and preparation.

Finally, a word of thanks to the many people who have stimulated us with their ideas. In presenting the many activities in this book, we hope very much that you will be encouraged to work with your children and to produce your own variations and ideas.

Thomas and Petra Berger

1. Spring

Magic-wool Mother Earth and flower children

Materials

- ✪ 12 pipe-cleaners
- ✪ Unspun sheep's wool
- ✪ Coloured magic wool

You will need four pipe-cleaners to make the head, arms and the upper body of each figure (Figure 1.1).

1. Make the arms by folding two of the pipe-cleaners in half.

2. Twist them together.

3. To make the head and upper body, take a third pipe-cleaner and twist it round the arms.

4. Twist a fourth pipe-cleaner round the head and body to strengthen it.

5. Tease out the unspun sheep's wool until it is very thin and twist it as tightly as possible round the arms. Keep doing this until they are thick enough. You will need more wool for Mother Earth than for the two small flower children. Now begin winding wool round the head, using thin tufts to ensure that the head becomes round. Make the head bigger than the length of the pipe-cleaner, as in step 5 (Figure 1.1). Unwashed sheep's wool has the advantage that the greasy wool binds together as it is wound round. If you don't have any, wind a thread over the wool from time to time to keep it firmly in place. Wind wool on to the lower body in the same way.

Use coloured magic wool to dress the doll. Tease out this wool as thinly as possible and wind it over the sheep's wool. Keep on doing this layer by layer until you can no longer see the sheep's wool and the doll is the desired colour (Figure 1.2).

Display the dolls in a safe place in the living room. They are delicate and if you let children play with them too much the coloured magic wool will soon come away.

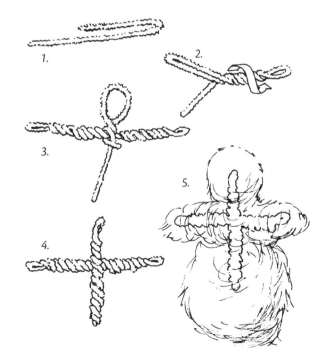

Opposite: 1.2 Mother Earth and flower children

1.1 Making Mother Earth

Felt flower children

Materials
- ✪ White or pink cotton knit
- ✪ Unspun sheep's wool
- ✪ Coloured magic wool
- ✪ Pieces of felt in various colours

Follow the diagram in Figure 1.4.

1. For the head take a piece of cotton knit 8 × 8 cm (3 × 3 in). Make a little ball of unspun wool, about 2 cm (3/4 in) in diameter, and place it in the centre of the piece of cotton.

2. Fold the cotton round the ball of wool and tie it at the neck.

3. For the body of the flower children you need a tube of felt. Take a rectangle of felt and sew two sides together. The length and width of the body is different for each kind of flower child (Figures 1.5–1.8).

4. Gather in one of the open ends to make the neck. Stuff the loose material of the head into the gathered end of the tube, and sew the neck and tube-body together.

The doll will now stand as it is, but you can fill the tube with unspun wool and sew a round piece of felt the same colour as the tube to the bottom.

This completes the basic form of all the flower children. Now follow the details according to the kind of flower.

1.3 Felt flower children

1.4 Making felt flower children

10

Crocus

For the body take a piece of green felt 6 × 6 cm (2¹/4 × 2¹/4 in) and follow the instructions on page 10.

1. For the collar take a piece of light purple felt 10 × 3.5 cm (4 × 1¹/2 in) and cut it out using the pattern in Figure 1.5. Gather in the upper edge and sew the collar round the neck.

2. Do the same with the cap, which can be a darker purple. Gather in the felt where indicated so the cap sits well on the head.

Give the flower child some hair using magic wool before securing the cap on to the head with a few stitches. Then stitch the top edge of opposite pairs of petals together.

Snowdrop

The snowdrop's body is 6 cm (2¹/4 in) high and 7 cm (2³/4 in) wide. Follow the instructions on page 10.

1. Cut out the light green collar (Figure 1.6), gather it where shown and sew it on to the body.

2. The snowdrop's cap consists of three separate white petals. Sew the tops of the petals on to a little stalk of light green felt (step 3).

Give the flower child some hair using white magic wool or unspun sheep's wool before sewing on the cap with a few stitches.

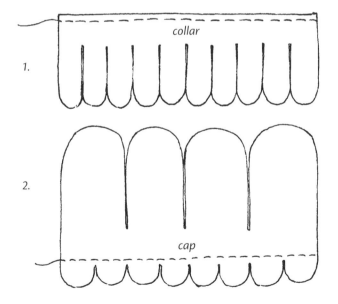

1.5 Crocus

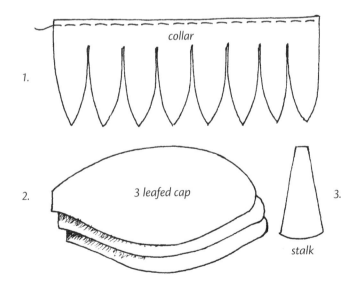

1.6 Snowdrop

Tulip

The tulip's body is 5.5 cm (2½ in) high and 10 cm (4 in) wide. Follow the instructions on page 10.

1. Cut out the red collar (Figure 1.7), gather it around the top and sew it on to the body.

2. The tulip child has a cap made of six separate red petals. Sew the first two petals to the side of the head. Gather in the remaining four petals where shown.

3. Then sew them on to the head overlapping each other.

Give the tulip pink hair.

Daffodil

The body of the daffodil is about 5 cm (2 in) high and 10 cm (4 in) wide. Follow the instructions on page 10.

1. Cut out the yellow collar (Figure 1.8), gather it round the top and sew it on to the body.

2. Give the flower child yellow hair before sewing on the cap. The daffodil's cap has two parts. First sew the gathered yellow petal wreath on to the head.

3. Cut out a round piece from dark yellow felt to make the heart of the flower. Cut into the disc in two places and sew it up so that it bulges out. Sew the heart on to the crown of the head.

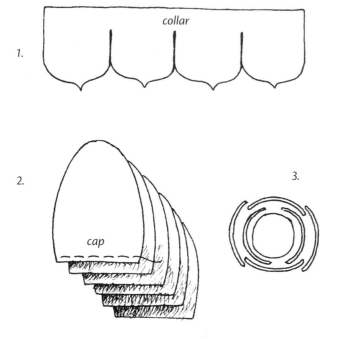

1.7 Tulip

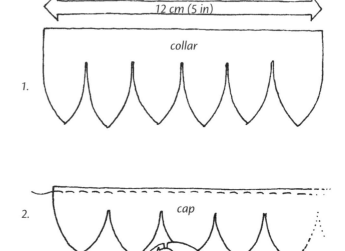

1.8 Daffodil

Modelling-wax transparency

Materials

- ✪ Pane of glass or perspex
- ✪ Modelling wax (such as Stockmar) in various colours
- ✪ Decorating wax (such as Stockmar) in various colours
- ✪ Hot-water bottle

This transparency is made on glass or perspex. Perspex has the advantage that it is a light-weight substance and you can hang up the transparency immediately by simply drilling small holes in the corners. With glass you will generally have to give it a lead frame with a hook to hang it up.

You can of course create a transparency freely, but if you haven't had much practice it is better to first make a sketch on paper. If you make the sketch the same size as your glass or perspex, you can stick it to the back of the pane and follow it. Don't let the drawing become too intricate. You can vary the picture as it develops.

Modelling wax is a coloured transparent wax which softens when kneaded gently; the softened wax is then easy to shape and can be pressed straight on to the pane. Stockmar decorating wax comes in thin strips and can be applied directly.

Take small pieces of wax because they are quicker to soften and you can cover large areas more easily.

As soon as you put the wax on to the glass or perspex it cools down and becomes hard, making it difficult to spread into a thin layer. You may find it helpful to keep the glass or perspex warm by laying it on a hot-water bottle.

From time to time hold up the pane to the window to see how it will look with light shining through it.

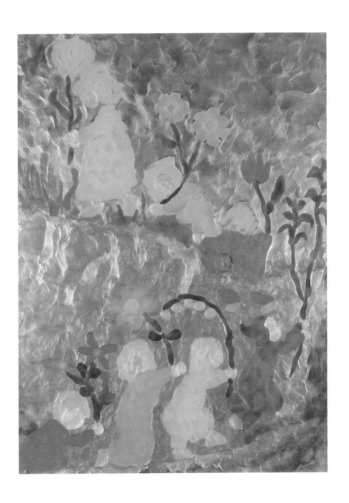

1.9 Modelling-wax transparency

Magic-wool picture

Materials
- ⊛ Cambric or other roughly woven fabric
- ⊛ Magic wool

Magic wool is fine carded sheep's wool which is available in many different colours. The wool will stick by itself on to a rough backing such as cambric or ribbed velvet.

First select a suitable colour of cambric, depending on the colours of wool you are going to use.

Hem round the edges of the cambric and lay the cloth on to a table, on a board, or secure it straight on to the wall.

Tease out the magic wool thinly, shape the wool and press it on to the backing. The thicker the magic wool the more intense the colours will be (Figure 1.10).

You can always re-shape part of the picture as it is easy to remove the wool from the backing. This is what makes magic wool so flexible — you can always change the picture, for instance, with the seasons.

If you are not intending to change the picture or want it as a gift, secure the tufts of magic wool with a few stitches.

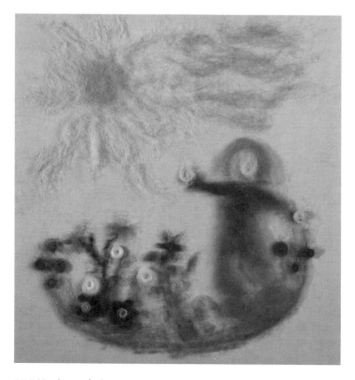

1.10 Magic-wool picture

Palm Sunday branches

Materials

- ✪ Branches
- ✪ Crêpe-paper
- ✪ Green sprigs of box tree (optional)
- ✪ Button thread, thin wire or florist's wire
- ✪ Cane
- ✪ Cockerel made of dough or paper
- ✪ Dried fruits: raisins, dried apples, dried apricots

1.11 Branch with round hoop

Processing with Palm Sunday branches is a very ancient custom in memory of Christ's entry into Jerusalem, when people took branches from the trees and laid them in his path.

In the past in Europe each region had its own model of Palm Sunday branch. Here we have two basic forms: with a round hoop and in the form of a cross. The symbol of the cross, as a reference to the crucifixion, can be difficult for little children to understand. For them a branch with a hoop is a sign of approaching spring, the circle being a symbol of the sun and light.

Continued overleaf

1.12 Cross-shaped branch

Branch with a round hoop

In the Palm Sunday branch shown in Figure 1.11 the stick is wrapped in light green crêpe-paper and decorated with dark green crêpe-paper.

Make sure that the branch is not too heavy. For little children don't make the stick longer than the child's arm.

Make a hoop about 30–40 cm (12–15 in) in diameter from cane and tie the ends firmly.

Let the children help with making and decorating the Palm Sunday sticks.

Decorate the hoop with streamers of crêpe-paper and dried fruits.

Finally bind the hoop to the stick with strong twine or thin wire, and put the cockerel in its place on top.

Finally you can decorate the branch with an orange into which box twigs have been inserted. Cut the top of the branch to a point so that the Palm Sunday cockerel can sit there. For instructions on baking a dough cockerel see page 23.

Cross-shaped branch

Find two suitable branches, with the horizontal branch half the length of the vertical branch. Notch both branches lightly where they are to cross and tie them together with thin wire or strong twine.

Put it in a stable vase or in a box filled with sand so that it will stand upright while you decorate it.

The Palm Sunday branch in Figure 1.12 is partially decorated with foliage from a box bush. (Many hedges are box, as it remains green throughout the year.) Take care when binding on the box twigs to keep them facing in the same direction because the underside and the topside of the leaves are different in colour.

Then wind coloured crêpe-paper around the horizontal branch, leaving just the ends showing a brush of box twigs.

Now hang streamers of crêpe-paper on to the horizontal branch. As shown in Figure 1.12 the strips of crêpe-paper (about 2 cm, 3/4 in wide) have been nicked on each side to allow more lively movement.

1.13 Baked dough cockerel

Paper cockerel

Children will soon eat the dough cockerel on top of the Palm Sunday branch, making it look rather bare! So get them to first make a paper cockerel.

From the card, cut out two cockerels with good fat bellies and a thin strip of about 2 cm (³/4 in) wide.

Let the children colour the two cockerels so that one is the mirror image of the other, as they will later be stuck together.

Make a little tube from the strip of card, which will fit over the point of the branch.

1. Stick the top edges of the cockerels together (Figure 1.15).

2. Insert the little tube in between the bottom edges, and glue it in place.

As soon as the dough cockerel has disappeared the paper cockerel can take its place on top of the branch!

1.14 Paper cockerel

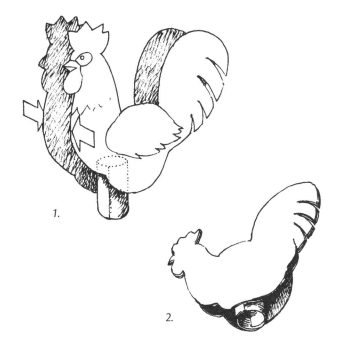

1.15 Making a paper cockerel

17

Easter trees

Find suitable branches for this Easter tree. Figure 1.16 shows suggested measurements.

Notch the places where the branches cross and tie them securely with strong thread or wire.

Decorate the tree with sprigs of box. It helps to put the tree in a stable vase or a box with sand.

Now carefully hang the blown-out eggs on to the tree: on the highest branch hang one egg on each side, on the middle branch two eggs and on the lowest branch three eggs on each side.

Leave the tree to stand in the vase or pot or fix it in a wooden base to keep it upright. Alternatively, put the tree in a box with early spring flowers.

Or you could try making the following version instead.

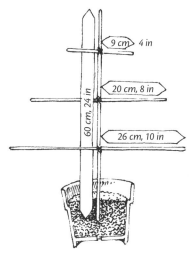

9 cm, 4 in

20 cm, 8 in

60 cm, 24 in

26 cm, 10 in

1.16 Measurements for Easter tree

Easter branches

You can make a very festive Easter decoration for a room by hanging coloured blown-out eggs on a branch or two.

Four weeks before Easter select suitable branches with buds and put them in water in a vase in a warm room. By Easter the buds will have opened and fresh green leaves will have come out.

At Easter decorate the branches with some beautifully decorated blown-out eggs.

1.17 Easter tree

Opposite:1.18 Easter branches

Growing cress

Sowing cress in a box lets children see plants sprouting in spring. After just one to two days, cress will sprout and after about a week it will be ready for eating.

Moisten the earth in the box well.

Spread the cress-seed evenly over the soil, and if your house is very dry cover the box with a thin plastic sheet.

In the warm humid atmosphere of the box the seeds should soon sprout. Take away the plastic once the seeds have sprouted.

Now the children can watch the cress grow daily until a tiny leaf appears on the end of each stalk. Make sure that the soil remains damp.

As a decoration for the Easter table you can also sow the cress in an eggshell.

Remove the top of a boiled egg carefully. To get a smooth round edge, first score gently round the eggshell with a fine metal saw and then break the shell carefully. The rest of the shell makes a little container which can be filled with earth and used to plant the seeds.

1.19 Eggshell with cress

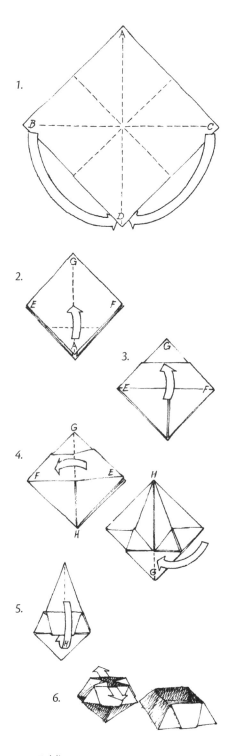

1.20 Folding an eggcup

Eggcups

Materials

- ✪ Toilet roll tubes
- ✪ Coloured paper
- ✪ Glue

Take an empty toilet roll and cut it into several rings 1.5–2 cm (³/4 in) wide.

Stick some coloured tissue or other paper on to the rings. Alternatively stick white paper on to the rings and let the children colour them. In this way children can make their own eggcups for Easter.

Folding an eggcup

Materials

- ✪ Square sheets of paper about 12 × 12 cm (5 × 5 in)
- ✪ Glue

Fold a sheet of paper in half in both directions. Open it out, turn it over, and repeat diagonally (Figure 1.20).

1. Bring the four corners together by folding B and C simultaneously on to point D. Point A will follow on top.

2. Fold point A to the line EF.

3. Then fold along EF. Turn over and repeat with point D.

4. Fold the top point F across to E and the lower point E to point F. Turn the whole thing round 180° so that point G comes to the bottom. Fold points F and E to the centre line. Repeat this for the back.

5. Fold point H to the bottom and tuck the point in as shown. Do the same for the back. Now the eggcup is almost finished.

6. Open out the top carefully so that the point at the bottom gradually disappears and becomes the base of the eggcup.

You can make the folded eggcup from coloured origami paper or from a sheet of white paper which the children have painted or coloured beforehand. In this case start with the coloured side of the sheet face up, and at the first stage, fold the coloured side into itself. The small square is white now, but the coloured side will end up on the outside.

1.21 Homemade eggcups

Baked dough figures

Dough recipe

Ingredients

- Approximately 500 g (1 lb) white or wholemeal flour or a mixture of both
- $1/2$ tablespoon of yeast dissolved in 300 ml (10 fl oz) lukewarm milk (not more than 30°C, 85°F)
- 50 g ($1^3/4$ oz) hard butter
- $1/2$ tablespoon salt
- 3 tablespoons sugar
- $1/2$ tablespoon aniseed

The recipe will make eight hares, or nests, or little men, and so on.

Keep about 100 g (4 oz) of flour back and put the rest into a bowl. Make a hole in the middle and pour the yeast mixture into it. Stir from the middle outwards taking in some of the flour to make a sloppy paste.

Cut the butter up into very thin slices and lay these on to this yeast mixture. Sprinkle the salt, sugar and aniseed over the butter. Put the bowl into a plastic bag and allow the mixture to rise to twice its volume at room temperature; this can take 20 minutes or more.

Take half of the flour which you have kept back. Sprinkle it over the mixture and at the same time work it into the mixture with the salt, sugar, aniseed and the butter which in the meantime has become soft.

Empty this loose dough on to a board sprinkled with flour and knead it (not too long) until it no longer sticks to your hand and feels firm but still soft and elastic. Knead the dough with the heel of your hand giving it a quarter turn now and again.

Put the dough back into the bowl, place in a fridge or cool place, and allow it to rise to about twice its volume. This will take three to four hours. Cold dough can be shaped better.

The forming of the risen dough is described in the sections that follow.

To finish off, pre-heat the oven. Before baking, brush the figures with loosely beaten egg or with egg yolk lightly whisked with some milk.

Bake for about 20 minutes at 225°C (435°F, gas mark 7) in the middle of the oven.

Palm Sunday cockerel

Make dough as in the recipe. Divide the risen dough into eight portions and roll out each portion to a strip about 18 cm (7 in) long.

Bend the strips round as you lay them on a baking tray, making the tail piece a bit shorter than the head-piece (Figure 1.22).

Make sure that there is enough space between each portion to allow for rising and above all make the figures *thin*; when they rise they will become thicker.

With a sharp pair of scissors cut twice into the dough to make the beak, pull out this piece and smooth off the cut.

Cut into both ends to make the comb and the tail and indicate the wings with single cuts.

Finally take a sharp knife and make a hole for the eye and put a raisin or currant in the hole.

You can decorate the dough cockerel as you like with nuts or dried fruit, and add him to your Palm Sunday branch (page 15).

Little bread men

Make dough as in the recipe, and divide the risen dough into eight portions.

1. Make each portion into a pear shape (Figure 1.23).

2. With a sharp knife cut slits to form arms and legs. Notch the eye sockets and insert two raisins to make the eyes.

3. Take a hard-boiled decorated egg, place it on the man's stomach and fold his arms over it. Only use eggs which have been coloured in a plant-dye bath, otherwise the dye may come off on the bread.

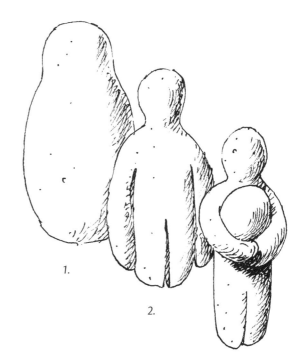

1.

2.

3.

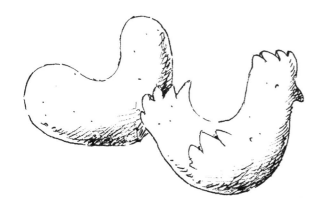

1.22 Making the cockerel

1.23 Making the bread men

Fruit-cake Easter hare

For this you will need a special two-part baking mould (Figure 1.24) in the shape of a hare or lamb (to hold 1/2 litre, 1 pint).

Ingredients

- ✪ 200 g (7 oz) wholemeal flour
- ✪ 1/2 tablespoon yeast dissolved in 100 ml (3 1/2 fl oz) milk
- ✪ Approximately 50–75 g (2 oz) hard butter
- ✪ 1/2 teaspoon salt
- ✪ 25 g (1 oz) cane sugar or syrup, dissolved in 1 egg yolk in half an eggshell of water
- ✪ Grated peel of half a lemon
- ✪ Approximately 60 g (2 oz) sliced stoned dates

Put the flour into a bowl and make a hollow in the middle. Pour the yeast mixture into the hollow and stir it with some of the flour into a runny paste. Lay the butter in thin slices on top and sprinkle with the salt.

Put the bowl into a plastic bag and allow it to stand at room temperature until bubbles appear in the mixture (20 minutes or longer).

Pour the egg-sugar syrup over the butter which has become soft and add the grated lemon peel. Stir and beat from the middle outwards to a smooth moist dough for 5 minutes.

Mix in the dates, put the bowl back into the plastic bag and allow the dough to rise to twice its volume. At room temperature this will take at least two hours and it does not matter if it takes longer.

Take the baking mould apart and grease the two halves with softened butter. Sprinkle flour over it and knock out the surplus flour.

Fill the moulds making sure that the ears and head are well filled before closing them together. Put the mould on a baking tray into a pre-heated oven.

Bake for about 30 minutes at 190°C (375°F, gas mark 5) on the bottom rack.

After removing from the oven, leave the mould closed for 5 minutes, then free the edges with a knife before carefully opening. Put the hare or lamb on to a rack to cool off.

Shortly before serving, cut the base level so that the animal will stand, and sprinkle with icing sugar.

1.24 Baking moulds for the hare

Knotted cloth hare

The symbol of the Easter hare is ancient. In Germanic mythology the hare brings the new seeds of life (eggs) to the earth. The hare has no burrow and does not live in herds. It sleeps under the open sky and leaves its young in sheltered places. In fairy tales we often see the hare rescuing other animals by sacrificing itself.

Materials
- ⭐ Soft square piece of cloth

1. Fold the cloth over diagonally, as shown in Figure 1.26.

2. Tie a loose knot in one end.

3. Then bring the other end through the loop of the knot to make two ears.

4. Pull the knot a bit tighter, pull the whole thing out a bit and there you have the hare (Figure 1.25).

1.25 Knotted cloth hare

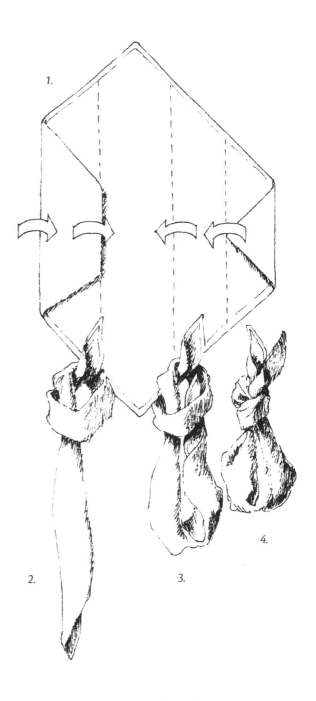

1.26 Making the knotted cloth hare

Pompom animals

Chicks

Materials

- ✪ Stiff cardboard
- ✪ Pair of compasses
- ✪ Large darning needle
- ✪ Yellow or white knitting yarn
- ✪ Scraps of orange felt
- ✪ Button thread

Each little chick is made of two pompoms, one large and one small.

Take the compasses and draw the following circles on the cardboard: two small ones with a radius of 18 mm (3/4 in) with a tiny circle inside of about 5 mm (1/4 in) radius; two circles with a radius of 26 mm (1 in) with a little circle with a radius of 17 mm (3/4 in) inside.

1. Cut out the circles so that you get rings with a hole in the middle. Cut a slit in the rings in one place (Figure 1.29).

2. Take a strong thread (or wool, if it is strong enough) and make a double loop. Lay the loop on one of the cardboard rings and lay the second ring of the same size on top of it, ensuring the cuts in the rings don't lie on top of each other. Let the ends of the loop hang down outside the rings.

3. Wind the wool loosely (by hand or with a darning needle) round the rings until the hole in the centre is filled up.

4. Push a scissor blade between the two rings and cut the wool round the outside. Draw the loop, which was laid between the rings, tight and tie it up firmly. Do not cut the ends of the loop yet.

You can now carefully remove the rings so that they can be used again, and trim the pompom.

Make the other pompom in the same way and tie the two together with the loose loop-threads.

Finally cut out one or two orange felt triangles and tie them to the smaller pompom for the beak.

Of course you can make a whole brood of chicks!

1.27 Pompom chicks

1.28 Pompom rabbit

Rabbits

Materials
- ✪ Stiff cardboard
- ✪ Pair of compasses
- ✪ Brown knitting yarn
- ✪ Scraps of brown felt
- ✪ Large darning needle

The smaller ring has a radius of 21 mm (^{7}/8 in) and a hole of 7 mm (^{1}/4 in); the larger ring has a radius of 35 mm (1 ^{3}/8 in) and a hole of 13 mm (^{1}/2 in).

The rabbits are made in the same way as the chicks described on page 26.

Tie the pompoms together, cut out two ears from some felt and sew them on to the head. For the eyes take two black beads and sew them loosely to the head.

With these larger rings you can also use unspun brown wool. For this, card the wool in thin long wisps and then wind them round the card. Rabbits made of unspun sheep's wool have to be well trimmed.

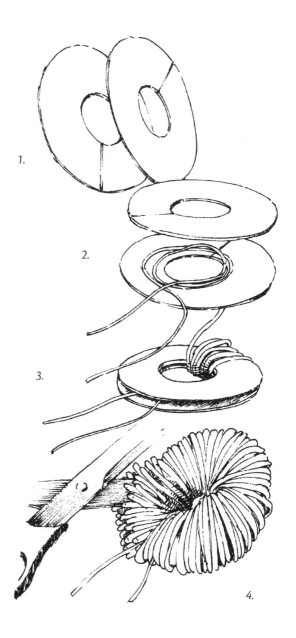

1.29 Making pompoms

Knitted chicken

Materials

- ✪ Yellow yarn
- ✪ Knitting needles 2–2.5 mm (US size 1)
- ✪ Unspun sheep's wool
- ✪ Red wool

1. Cast on 16 stitches and knit each row to form a square. Cast off.

2. Fold the piece over diagonally and sew up one of the sides (Figure 1.30). Sew the other side only halfway up. Fill the body with unspun wool and finish sewing up the side.

3. Shape the chicken by running a thread from the point of the underside round the hen's middle. Draw in the thread lightly, and secure: this will pull the head and tail up.

Use red wool to sew button-hole stitch to make the comb and gills (Figure 1.31).

Make the eyes using a stitch of darker wool or a bead.

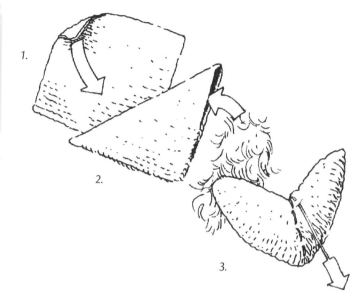

1.30 Making a knitted chicken

1.31 Knitted chicken

1.32 Knitted hare egg cosy

Egg cosies

Knitted hare egg cosy

Materials

- ✪ Brown knitting yarn
- ✪ Knitting needles 3–3.5 mm (US size 3)
- ✪ Unspun sheep's wool
- ✪ Brown and pink felt
- ✪ Embroidery thread
- ✪ 2 beads for eyes

Cast on 20–28 stitches depending on the thickness of the wool. The length should go round an eggcup comfortably. If your yarn is very thin, double it. Knit a piece of about 36 plain rows. Do not cast off, but string the stitches on to the knitting yarn, pull tight and break off.

Sew up the long side to make a tube. Stuff it one third full with some unspun wool to make the head. Tie up the neck with a length of wool and shape the head so that the nose runs to a point.

For the ears use two pieces of felt. Make the pink felt piece a little smaller and sew it on to the brown felt. Pinch the felt ears together at the bottom and sew them on to the head.

Embroider the eyes or use two beads. Finally embroider the nose and give the hare a few whiskers (Figure 1.32).

Felt egg cosy

Materials

- ✪ Pieces of coloured felt
- ✪ Embroidery thread

Figure 1.33 shows an egg cosy decorated with flowers. The flowers are cut out from felt and sewn on to the background. Of course this kind of egg cosy can be made in all sorts of different ways, also by working just with embroidery thread on the felt.

Cut out two pieces according to the pattern in Figure 1.34.

Decorate one or both sides in your own way and sew the two pieces together.

1.33 Felt egg cosy

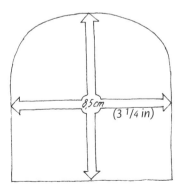

1.34 Pattern for felt egg cosy

Felt hen egg cosy

Materials

- ✪ Yellow felt in two shades
- ✪ Red felt
- ✪ Unspun sheep's wool
- ✪ 2 beads for eyes
- ✪ Embroidery thread

Cut out the body twice, the wings twice, the beak twice, and the comb once according to the pattern in Figure 1.36.

Sew the wings on to the body. Then sew the two halves of the hen's body together using buttonhole-stitch, stitching the comb between the two parts. Finish off the bottom also with buttonhole-stitch.

Sew the two red beaks into place and fill the head with some unspun wool.

Finally sew the beads into place as eyes.

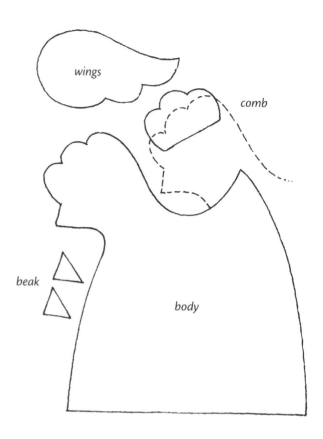

1.36 Pattern for felt hen egg cosy

1.35 Felt hen egg cosy

Easter-bunny puppets

Finger puppet

Materials

- ✪ Thin knitting wool in a suitable rabbit colour
- ✪ Knitting needle 2 mm (US size 0)
- ✪ Unspun sheep's wool
- ✪ 2 beads for eyes
- ✪ Embroidery thread
- ✪ Mini chocolate egg

1.37 Finger puppets

Cast on 20 stitches and knit 20 rows, 1 row plain 1 row purl for the body. Then knit 10 rows, 1 row purl and 1 row plain (reversing the pattern) to make the head.

Do not cast off, but run the stitches on to the knitting yarn. Pull the yarn tight and break off.

Sew up the long edge, so that the head is ribbed on the outside. Fill the head with unspun wool, turning the front edge outwards a little to make a nose. Tie up the neck with a length of wool.

For the ears cast on 8 stitches and knit 10 rows, 1 row plain 1 row purl. On the eleventh row decrease by knitting two stitches together four times. Knit the twelfth row purl. On the thirteenth row decrease by knitting two stitches together twice. Cast off.

Sew up the sides and sew the ears on to the head keeping the seams at the back.

For the rucksack cast on 16 stitches and knit 8 rows plain. Run the stitches on to the knitting yarn, pull the yarn tight and break off.

Sew the rucksack on to the back, securing the yarn crosswise with a few stitches to make the straps.

Embroider a nose, give the bunny some whiskers and sew the beads in place for eyes (Figure 1.37).

Finally place a mini chocolate egg in the rucksack.

Glove puppet

Materials
- ✪ Fabric, preferably cotton knit
- ✪ Pink and brown felt
- ✪ Unspun sheep's wool
- ✪ Embroidery thread

Select a suitable piece of fabric and cut out the head, body and ears, each twice, using the pattern in Figure 1.39.

First sew the pink fronts on to the ears, inside out and turn them. The bottoms should still be open.

Sew the eyes on to the separate halves of the head. Sew the halves together inside out, leaving the neck open. Turn right side out.

Then embroider the pink inside of the paws on to the two pieces of the body. Sew together the body pieces inside out leaving the bottom and the neck open. Turn the body right side out, and hem the bottom.

Now all the separate pieces can be sewn together. First sew the head into the neck of the body and then the ears on to the head.

Finish off the Easter hare by filling the head with some unspun wool and make a hole in the wool with your finger so that later a finger will fit in when the hare is played with. Finally give the animal an embroidered nose and whiskers.

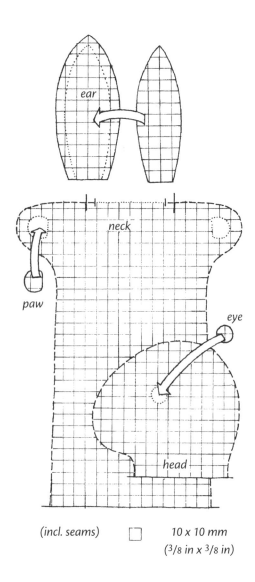

(incl. seams) ☐ 10 x 10 mm
(3/8 in x 3/8 in)

1.39 Pattern for glove puppet

1.38 Glove puppet

Decorating Easter eggs

The tradition of decorating eggs goes back to before the beginnings of recorded history. The egg was seen as the symbol for germinating power and new life.

There are many ways of decorating Easter eggs. The method depends on what you want to do with the eggs. Are they going to be eaten or just used for decoration?
If they are to be eaten, we can decorate boiled eggs before they come on to the Easter breakfast table or are hidden in the garden.

For decoration, blown-out eggs can be hung on an Easter tree or blossoming branch, for the whole time from Easter to Ascension. You can even keep blown-out eggs carefully for another year.
For some of the methods, for example with batik, you will have to immerse the egg in a liquid. This is not really suitable for blown-out eggs, and is better on eggs that have been very hard boiled (half an hour or more), so that they don't rot so quickly.

The quality of eggshells can vary greatly, so check that your shell is not too thin (it may crack or break while being boiled or blown out) and check that the surface is nice and smooth.
White eggs are the best for decorating but they are often hard to obtain.

Eggshells are always a bit greasy. To enable the paint or colouring to stick properly the grease should first be removed with some vinegar or washing-up liquid.

Blowing out eggs

Make a hole in the top and bottom of the egg with a pin or an egg-pricker.

These holes are still too small to let you blow the egg out, so take two large round nails, one about 2 mm (1/12 in) thick and the other about 4 mm (3/8 in) thick. Sharpen the points of the nails so that they can serve as a kind of drill.

Make one of the holes in the egg a little larger (the hole you blow through) and use the thin nail at the other end (Figure 1.40).

Blow the egg out over a jar (use it for scrambled eggs or omelettes), then rinse out the inside of the eggshell a little by letting some water flow in through the hole and blowing it out again. This is to ensure that no residue is left in the shell. Make sure that no water remains in the shell.

Figure 1.41 shows a very simple gadget, a Blas-fix, which makes the blowing-out of eggs much easier by only requiring one hole and no blowing.

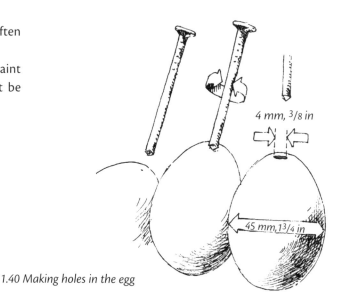

4 mm, 3/8 in

45 mm, 1 3/4 in

1.40 Making holes in the egg

Batik variation

When eggs have to be left for some time submerged in a bath of hot dye, make the larger hole bigger with the thicker nail. This is done by twisting the nail slowly and applying light pressure, so the sharp edges cut into the egg without breaking it. The dye can now enter the eggshell and it stays submerged.

Hanging up eggs

1. After the egg has been decorated tie the end of a length of thread firmly around the middle of half a matchstick (or piece of wire) and poke the match with the thread through the hole in the egg. Now pull the thread carefully and the match will come to rest across the egg and will not come out.

2. If the egg has two slightly larger holes you can run a thin ribbon right through the egg and tie a bow in it at the bottom.

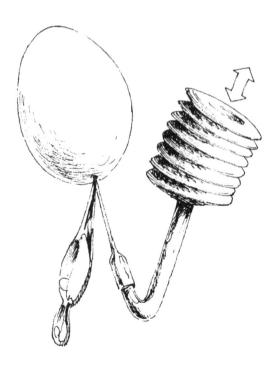

1.41 Blas-fix egg blower

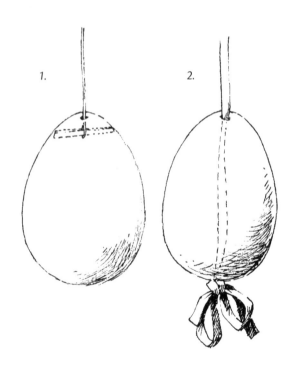

1.42 Hanging up eggs

Using pencils or wax crayons

Decorating eggs with coloured pencils or wax crayons is very simple (Figure 1.43). For children thick crayons or block crayons are best. Even the smallest children can take part.

Note that blown-out eggs are very fragile and can easily be squashed by young children. Hard-boiled eggs are more suitable.

1.43 Egg decorated with crayons

Using plant dyes

Materials
⭐ Tea, coffee, camomile, onion skin, juice from spinach, beetroot and so on.

Everyday plant products used in the kitchen are suitable for dying eggs, such as tea leaves, coffee, camomile and onion skin, or vegetables like spinach and beetroot. Exotic plants and insect dyes, such as turmeric from India, sandalwood from Africa, or cochineal from the West Indies will also produce beautiful colours. Some of these products are sold as egg dyes. In general they need only a short time on the boil.

Put the material to make the dye into a pot of cold water and bring to the boil. Then carefully immerse the thoroughly cleaned egg into the boiling water. Of course white eggs will take on better colours than brown eggs.

With some materials, like coffee and tea, first bring the water to boiling before adding the material. Leave to boil for a short time before immersing the eggs.

You will have to experiment a bit, at first especially, with the length of time for boiling.

Plant dyes cannot be used indefinitely. After five or six eggs have been boiled in them the colour begins to fade. Use a small saucepan and make sure that the eggs are fully immersed, or turn them over regularly.

You can get a whole range of colours, which can be made more intense by a dash of vinegar.

Light yellow: camomile flowers, marigold petals
Light brown: onion skin (5–10 minutes)
Dark brown: strong black tea or coffee
Red: beetroot juice is very good
Green: boiled liquid of spinach or nettles
Violet: huckleberries, grapes

Once the eggs have dried off thoroughly after their colour bath they can be rubbed with a cloth dipped in salad oil. This will give them a soft sheen and the colour will not rub off so easily.

The eggs on the Easter tree in Figure 1.17 were coloured with plant dyes.

Using paint

Materials
- Paints (watercolours, poster paint or plant dyes)
- Paintbrushes
- Wooden skewers or thin knitting needles
- Wire
- A little modelling wax

One of the difficulties in painting an egg is holding it without putting your fingers on the wet painted part, and being able to turn the egg round as you paint. There are several ways of overcoming this difficulty, as shown in Figure 1.45.

1. One simple way is to push a long wooden skewer (or thin knitting needle) through both holes and secure it with a bit of modelling wax.

2. Another way is to bend a bit of wire so that it acts like a pair of tongs with each end of the wire inserted in the holes of the egg.

3. Finally there are egg holders on the market which hold the egg. The holder comes with six different watercolours made of natural substances, which are safe for young children.

You can simply paint the egg or first put it into a colour bath to provide a background colour. Use the paint fairly thickly. If it's too thin, it will run.

Once the eggs are thoroughly dry apply a coat of varnish so that the colours will not subsequently run.

Using decorating wax

Materials
- Blocks of modelling wax (such as Stockmar) in various colours
- Strips of decorating wax (such as Stockmar) in various colours
- Sharp knife or skewer

Take a small piece of modelling wax and warm it by kneading it. When the wax has become soft apply it thinly to the egg, pressing it on firmly. Cut out the required shape with a knife or skewer.

You can peel off very thin strips of decorating wax with a knife. Apply them carefully to the egg and press on firmly. Because the wax is transparent you can apply several layers of different colours over each other as shown in Figure 1.44.

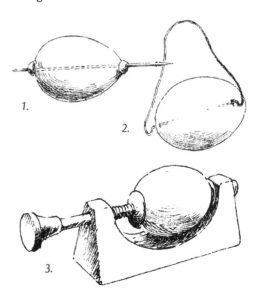

Opposite: 1.44 Eggs with decorating wax

1.45 Holding your egg

Scratching away colour

For this scratching-away technique it is important that the egg should have a strong shell. Of course you can also scratch out designs on hard-boiled eggs.

Start with an egg that has been strongly coloured using plant dyes and first sketch on your design with a fine pencil.

Now take a sharp craft knife. Scrape away several times to remove the colour completely and allow the plain white eggshell to become visible.

By not removing all the colour you will leave a lighter shade (Figure 1.47).

Potato stamping

By using a stamp you can keep repeating the same design so that you get a symmetrical effect. By using different colours and by turning the egg you can achieve interesting effects (Figure 1.48).

1. Cut a potato into several large pieces, each of them having one flat surface, as shown in Figure 1.46. Dry the potato with kitchen paper.

2 and 3. With a knife carve out a design in the flat surface and use the potato as a stamp.

Squeeze out some undiluted poster paint on to a flat surface, press the stamp into it and print on to the egg. Continue round the egg. If desired use different colours.

Allow the paint to dry thoroughly and coat with varnish.

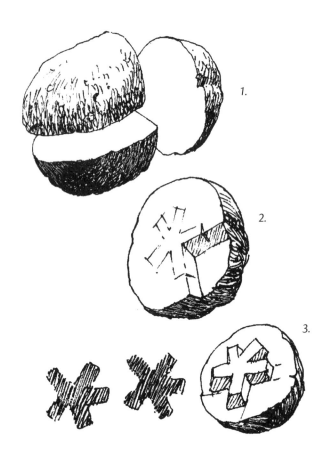

1.46 Potato stamping

1.47 Colour scratched away

1.48 Eggs decorated with potato stamps

Using trimmings and wool

Materials

- ✪ Fabric trimmings
- ✪ Glue
- ✪ Different coloured yarns
- ✪ Glue stick

Figure 1.50 shows how you can make very simple decorations with fabric trimmings. Just stick trimmings on to the egg with glue. Use quick-drying glue with a fine nozzle so that not too much glue goes on to the egg. Surplus glue makes unwanted shiny patches when dry.

Begin by using a glue stick: apply a little glue to the top (or bottom) making sure that you leave the hole open.

1. Press one end of the yarn into the glue and make a nice round loop. Press the loop well down and run the yarn carefully round the loop, applying a little glue as you go till you have gone round once or twice (Figure 1.49).

2. When changing colour, lay the new colour against the old one and run the yarn round the egg once. Pass the second colour over the yarn of the first, leaving the yarn of the first colour to hang down — which can be taken up again later. Always start new colours at the same place.

To make a symmetrically decorated egg, stick the yarns on alternately at the top and at the bottom until they meet in the middle.

Cut off the loose hanging yarns when the egg is finished and stick the cut-off ends down firmly.

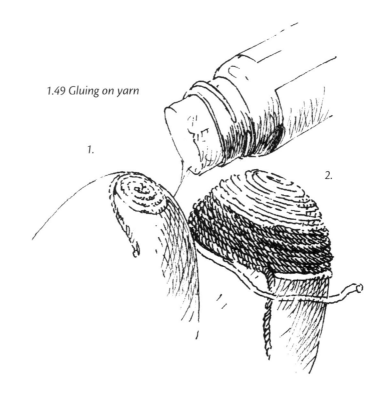

1.49 Gluing on yarn

1.

2.

Opposite: 1.50 Eggs with trimmings and wool

Using dried flowers and leaves

At Easter time there are hardly any flowers suitable for drying. Ideally use a flower press during the previous summer to make a collection of dried flowers for Easter (see page 61).

As an egg is only about 6 cm (2½ in) high, use small flowers and leaves.

Select those flowers, flower clusters and leaves which have strong silhouette forms or which are very regular in shape. A wreath of leaves round a stem can be very effective, or a highly indented leaf. Thin petals are easily torn when being stuck on to the egg.

Stick the flowers and leaves on to white or coloured eggs with a bit of glue. After gluing press the flowers and leaves flat with your hand and hold them in position until the glue dries (Figures 1.51–1.53).

1.52 and 1.53 More eggs decorated with dried flowers and leaves

1.51 Eggs decorated with dried flowers and leaves

Using quilling

Materials

- ✪ Quilling paper
- ✪ Quilling pen
- ✪ Tweezers
- ✪ Glue with a fine nozzle

Working with quilling paper is delicate work but it gives a lot of pleasure and the coloured rolls of paper can look very effective.

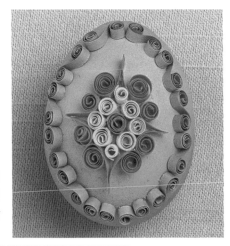

1.54 and 1.55 Eggs decorated with quilling

Quilling is an ancient craft using narrow strips of paper wound round the quill of a goose feather. A little slit was made in the end of the quill into which one end of the strip of paper was fitted.

Use strips of paper 3–4 mm ($^1/8$ in) wide. They usually come in lengths of 50 cm (20 in). Decide whether to take a half or a quarter length for your work.

Instead of the real quill of a goose feather, quilling pens are available. One end of the quilling paper is inserted in the slit of the quilling pen and the strip is wound round the pen. If you don't have a quilling pen you can use a cocktail stick. If you are expert in this technique you can even use a pin, for the smaller the hole inside, the better the result will be.

Once the strip has been wound right round the quill, finish off by sticking the end down with glue. As soon as you take the roll off the quill or cocktail stick, the strip will roll out to the stuck-on end so that you get this particular effect (Figure 1.6).

With an open spiral it is not necessary to stick the ends down. The spirals in Figures 1.54 and 1.55 show this. Of course there are plenty of variations and other forms possible.

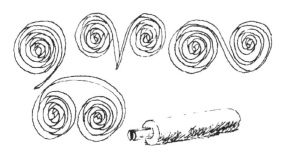

1.56 Quilling shapes

1.57–1.58 Eggs decorated with straw

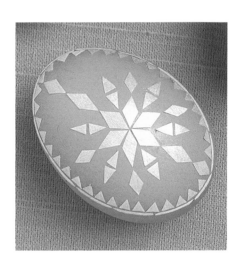

1.59–1.60 Eggs decorated with wood shavings

Using straw and wood shavings

Materials
- ✪ Craft straw
- ✪ Rolls of shavings
- ✪ Tweezers
- ✪ Sharp knife of pair of scissors
- ✪ Glue
- ✪ Zinc or perspex as a cutting board

Working with straw or shavings is a delicate job. The bits are often so tiny that you need tweezers to hold them.

Wood shavings are very pliable and thin and so easy to work. Straw by contrast is much stiffer but has a shiny surface: it must be soaked in water for half an hour before it can be split open and ironed flat. It is better to do this part of the work the day before and to press the ironed straw in a book to prevent it from curling.

The eggs in Figures 1.57 and 1.58 are decorated with straw while Figures 1.59 and 1.60 show eggs decorated with wood shavings.

On a piece of paper draw the oval shape of an egg and make a sketch of the design you wish to make. Working with straw is more satisfying with symmetrical designs.

Cut out the desired figures in their final shape and lay them out ready.

If you find it difficult to stick the shapes straight on to the egg you can first trace a few faint guiding lines on the egg with a sharp pencil.

Now start to stick the shapes on, using the tweezers if necessary. Apply glue with a fine nozzle so that your work is as neat as possible.

From time to time press the bits carefully on with your hand. As the egg progresses you can see whether the design requires any more to be added or even some parts to be left bare. Begin with simple designs, and only try more complex ones when you have built up some experience.

The pink egg in Figure 1.60 is plastered with squares. Such a design is difficult because squares and a round egg don't belong together. Make the front and back the same, and fiddle the sides a bit (as can be seen on the lower edge of the picture).

1.61 Batik eggs (see overleaf)

Batik eggs with flowers and leaves

Materials
- Dry brown onion skins
- Young leaves and flowers
- Old nylon stockings
- Thread

Take one or more simple little flowers or leaves, wet them and lay them on the unboiled egg. As long as they are damp they will stay in place.

Take as big an onion skin as possible and cover the leaf and the egg with it. Then wrap the egg in a number of onion skins until you can no longer see the egg. Put the whole thing into a nylon stocking and tie this up tightly round the egg so that the onion skins stay in place.

Make a bed of onion skins in a saucepan, and lay the egg in the nylon stocking on the bed. Fill the saucepan with water, bring to the boil, and leave it all to boil for about 10 minutes.

Allow the egg to cool off in the saucepan before taking it out of its wrapping. When the last onion skin and the leaves have been removed you will see that the egg has a brown colour while the shape of the leaves has been left.

To give the eggs a soft sheen you can rub them lightly with salad oil.

Alternatively the eggs can be dyed with textile dyes suitable for cold baths.

Czech and Ukrainian batik eggs

Decorating eggs with batik is an ancient folk art in Slavic countries, which is still practised today. There are significant differences in form and motif according to each country and region. The two eggs on the left of Figure 1.61 are Czech, and their main motifs are the sun and flowers. The two eggs on the right come from the Ukraine, where geometric forms are more common.

Materials
- Beeswax (thinned with paraffin if required)
- Candle
- A *tjanting* (*kiska*) or holder with a nail
- Vinegar
- Flannel cloth
- Elastic bands
- Batik dyes

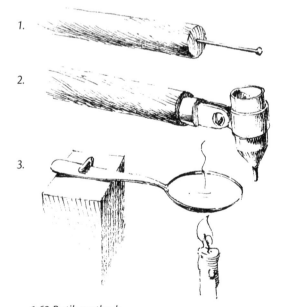

1.
2.
3.

1.62 Batik methods

This type of batik requires much patience and practice; in the beginning you can expect things to go wrong! It is best to start with very simple designs. Figure 1.63 shows a number of basic forms which of course can be developed further.

You can use both hard-boiled and blown-out eggs; the heavier boiled egg is easier to submerge in the dye bath.

Rub the egg clean with a cloth dipped in vinegar to remove any grease. After that always hold the egg with a cloth, as any grease from your hand will prevent the egg from taking on the dye.

1. The simplest batik pen is a round wooden stick with a nail stuck in it (Figure 1.62). This was used to make the patterns in this book.

2. You can also get a *tjanting* or *kiska*, which has a nozzle with a brass container for the liquid wax. *Tjantings* for cloth batik have a much smaller nozzle. By heating the container above a candle flame the wax will remain liquid.

Another option is to buy a special batik pen, which you hold in a candle flame until it is well heated and then dip it into a block of beeswax to produce a thin layer of liquid wax around the pen.

Finally you can apply the wax with the quill of a feather; the shape of the quill will determine the character of the design.

Heat the beeswax in a tin placed in a pan of boiling water (this prevents the wax from boiling excessively). If the wax is not runny enough, thin it with a little paraffin.

3. Use an old spoon held over a candle as a wax reservoir (Figure 1.62).

Applying the wax is a tricky job. You have to keep dipping the point of the nail into the liquid wax as you draw on the egg with the wax.

Aesthetically, an egg demands symmetry. Always begin the floral patterns in the middle and work your way outwards (see the egg on the far left in Figure 1.61). The same applies when you are making bands or garlands.

To start it can help to draw the design on the egg very lightly with a yellow or blue coloured pencil. Before you make lines or garlands which go right round the egg you can slip one or two elastic bands around as a marker.

Remember the areas covered in wax will remain white, while the uncovered areas will take on the colour.

Begin by making an egg with a single colour only. Draw the design on the egg with the wax pen. The wax will dry almost immediately.

The egg can now be immersed in the dye bath. The dye liquid must be cold otherwise the wax will melt. Keep the egg immersed until it has acquired the right intensity of colour. When you remove the egg from the dye you will see that the wax of the design has prevented the dye from colouring the egg there, so you will have a white design on a coloured background.

It is difficult to immerse a blown-out egg. You can run a stick or thin knitting needle through the egg (Figure 1.45) and pour the dye over the egg.

Warm the egg in the oven or with a hairdryer until the wax begins to melt, then wipe it off with paper tissues, leaving a thin protective layer on the egg.

You can also rub in a little oil, and the egg is finished.

Continued overleaf

To make batik eggs with several colours begin with the lightest colour. Draw a design in wax on the white egg and immerse the egg in the dye bath, for example in yellow.

If the wax were now to be removed you would get a white drawing on a yellow background; but now leave the wax on, and once the colour has dried make a fresh design, this time on the yellow background.

Now choose a darker dye bath, red for example. The result is a drawing in white and a drawing in yellow on a red background.

Make a new design on the red background and immerse the egg in a still darker dye bath, black for example. When the egg is removed, and the melting wax wiped away, a design emerges on the egg in white, yellow and red on a black background.

1.63 Basic patterns for batik

Concertina paper animals

Materials
- ✪ Thin card (about 150 gsm, 40 lb bond) in various colours
- ✪ Sharp knife or pointed scissors
- ✪ Glue

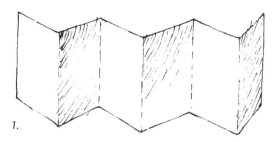

1.

There are many suitable subjects, but here we describe an Easter hare, a chicken and a cockerel.

Don't use card that's too thick and don't make too many folds because you will not be able to cut through the thickness. First look at the size of the card and how often it can be folded. If you have an even number of panels, this will give symmetry.

1. Cut out a strip of card and fold it in a concertina fashion (Figure 1.64).

2. Sketch out the required design on a piece of paper. Then copy this design on to the outside of the card or trace the design with carbon paper. It is important that your outline comes right up to the edges of the paper, keeping contact between the folds, otherwise the finished cut-out will fall apart.

3. Cut out the figures with scissors or a sharp knife. The cut-out can still be decorated or coloured in by children.

You can cut out two or more designs and set them up in front of each other to make a kind of story, as in Figure 1.66, where the hens come running up to the cockerel.

2.

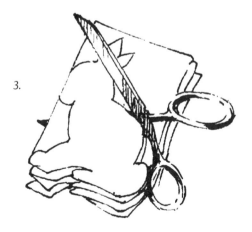

3.

1.64 Making a concertina rabbit

1.65 Concertina Easter rabbit

1.66 and 1.67 Concertina chickens

Origami animals

Chicken

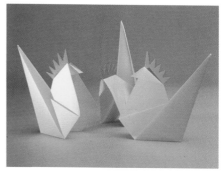

1.68 Origami chickens

1. Fold the sheet once across the diagonal so that point *B* comes on to point *C*, and open it again (Figure 1.69).

2. Now fold points *B* and *C* to the middle along the diagonal and stick them down with a tiny bit of glue.

3. Then fold point *D* to point *A*.

4. Turn the piece round so that points *E* and *F* are interchanged and make a vertical fold through *A* so that point *E* comes on to point *F*.

5. Draw corners *A* and *D* apart and make a new fold.

6. Press point *A* inwards so that you make a beak. Cut out a comb from a bit of cardboard and stick it in the fold which you have just made. Now the chicken can stand on the new fold. If we make fold *b* a bit smaller and fold *a* a bit bigger the chicken will stand on fold-line *a* and look as if she is pecking.

You can also give the chicken eyes.

Sheets of different sizes will result in a flock of different-sized hens.

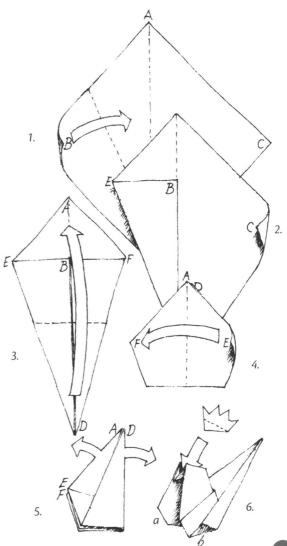

1.69 Folding an origami chicken

Hare

Materials
- ⊗ Sheets of coloured paper about 14 cm (5½ in) square
- ⊗ Glue

1. Fold the sheet once across the diagonal so that point *A* comes over point *D*. Open again.

2. Fold *A* and *D* to the middle along the diagonal and stick them together with a tiny bit of glue.

3. Fold *E* and *F* also to the diagonal and stick them with a tiny bit of glue.

4. Fold the piece over along the diagonal so that points *E* and *F* come to the outside as shown. Cut into the line *BC* from *B* a quarter of the total length *BC* and from *C* up to point *E*. Then cut into the line *EG* about half the distance *EG*.

5. This makes two points *C* and two points *B*. The Figure shows how point *C1* is folded upwards to make one of the two ears, while *B1* is folded forward to make one of the hind legs. Repeat with *C2* and *B2*.

6. Make an extra fold at the hind legs to emphasise them and to enable the hare to stand better.

Then you can let children colour the hare with crayons.

Here too you can vary the size of the sheets for different-sized hares.

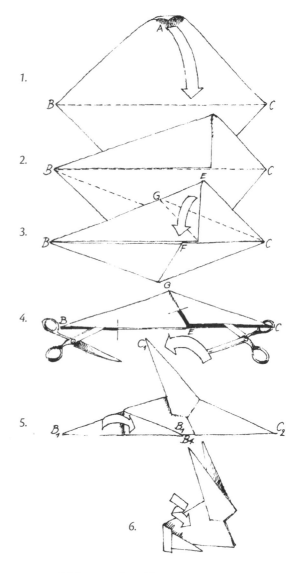

1.71 Folding an origami hare

1.70
*Origami
hare*

Swan

Materials
- Sheets of white paper about 12 cm (4³/4 in) square
- Glue

1. Fold the sheet once across the diagonal so that point *B* meets point *C* (Figure 1.73). Open again.

2. Fold *B* and *C* in to this diagonal fold.

3. Fold point *D* up to where points *B* and *C* come together. Fold *D* back so that the folded point is about a quarter of the length of the line along which it is folded.

4. Fold *E* and *F* to each other so that the point *D* that has just been folded comes to the outside. Work the point of *D* to the front, press the fold that you have thus made firmly, and your swan is finished.

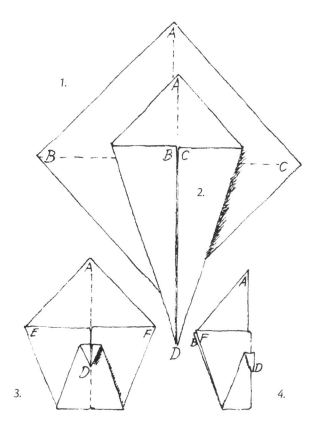

1.73 Folding an origami swan

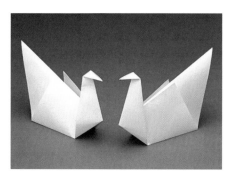

1.72 Origami swan

2. Summer

Tissue-paper flowers

Materials
- Tissue paper in various colours
- Copper wire (0.8 mm, 20 gauge)
- Glue
- Cotton wool
- Strong thread
- Small pointed pair of pliers
- Very thin wire (0.3 mm, 28 gauge)

The picture in Figure 2.1 shows a vase with a number of different flowers which can be made in three different ways. You can copy real flowers as exactly as possible, or you can freely use your imagination.

Stalk and heart

1. The stalk is the same for all these flowers. Take a piece of copper or steel wire (copper wire is more pliable). The length depends on the size of the vase you are going to use (Figure 2.2, page 56).

2. Using pliers, make a curl at one end of the wire, around which you can hook a piece of cotton wool. Lay it on a square piece of tissue paper. The colour of the tissue paper depends on the colour of the rest of the flower.

3. Fold the tissue paper around the cotton wool and secure it underneath.

4. For flowers with stamens in their hearts take a few pieces of very thin wire about 6–7 cm (2^1/2 in) long and tie a tiny bead on to the end of each wire. Join the stamens to each other by twisting the wires together. Attach this bundle on to the thicker wire by winding it round a loop a few times.

5. For flowers like the rose which have no visible heart, take a piece of wire and bend over at one end. Stick a bit of tissue paper over this end. This will give you a better hold when it comes to winding on the flower.

Basic flower

1. Choose a colour for the petals and cut out a strip from a sheet of tissue paper of this colour. The length (for the height of flower) can be 4–5 cm (1^1/2–2 in).

2. Fold the long strip in two and then again and so on until you reach the required width of the petal. This width can vary from 4 cm (1^1/2 in) for red and pink roses to 2 cm (^{3}/4 in) for the dark yellow flowers shown in Figure 2.1.

3. Cut one end of the folded pack into a rounded shape (Figure 2.3, page 56). Unfold the pack.

Stick one edge of the strip to the top of the stalk with a bit of glue. If you stick the strip on too low down you may find that when you come to wind on the petals, they stick too close together. Begin by ruching the petals together at the bottom and at the same time winding the strip round the wire, going progressively lower.

Once the strip has been fully wound round the wire stick down the end. Check whether the flower is filled out enough. If not, repeat the process with a half or possibly a whole strip.

Tie up the bottom of the petals with a bit of thread and finish off the stalk by wrapping a strip of green tissue paper round the wire.

Cut out some leaves. Stick them onto the stalk, making sure they are firmly glued at the bottom.

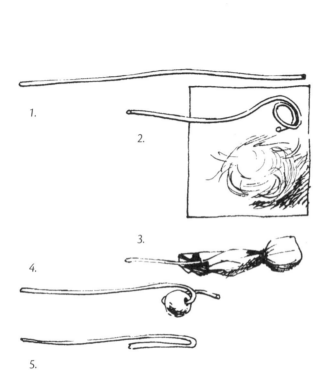

2.2 Making the stalk and heart

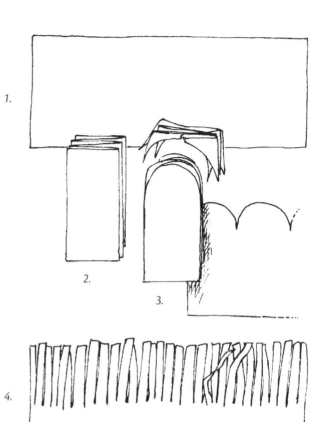

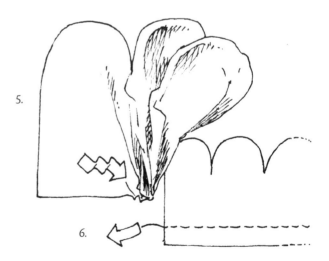

2.3 Making petals

Dahlias

To make dahlia-like flowers with petals consisting of very small strips, keep on folding the cut-out strip until you have the width of a petal, but remember that your scissors must be able to cut through the thickness of the pack.

4. Make cuts close together into one side (Figure 2.3). Finish as described above.

Six-petalled flowers

In Figure 2.1 the yellow flower sticking out above to the right has six petals. Depending on the size of the flower the petals have a width of about 2–4 cm (1–1^1/2 in).

Select three, four or five sheets of tissue paper in different or the same colours, whichever you prefer.

Lay the strips on top of each other before you begin to fold them (Figure 2.3, step 2). Concertina fold six petals. After cutting out the petals roundly (Figure 2.3, step 3) all the strips will be the same shape.

5. Unfold the strips and stick them together at the bottom so that they overlap (Figure 2.3).

6. Run a thread through all the petals one third up from the bottom. With this tacking thread the strips are now tied together, so you can cut off the bottoms about 5 mm (1/4 in) from the thread.

Stick the petals at each end of the strip together to make a round cylinder, strengthening it with a little strip of tissue paper of the right colour (or you can anticipate this by leaving a little strip on one of the ends when you cut it out).

Pull in the threads as tightly as possible and tie them together. Push the stalk through the flower and stick the petals to the heart of the flower. Open out the petals nicely.

Finish off the stem in the same way as the basic flower.

Flowers with separate petals

Fold a strip of tissue paper into a concertina pack and cut out the separate petals.

Stick the petals on, one by one, onto the paper under the heart of the flower (which has already been tied on). Each successive petal should come a little further up to overlap. Choose the number and colours of petals.

Once the last petal has been stuck on, secure them with a thread and they will splay out by themselves. If necessary, tug some out a little more.

Finish the flowers off as with the basic flower described on page 55.

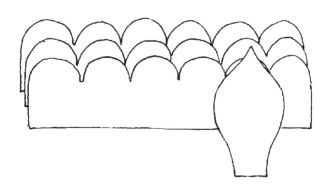

2.4 Making separate petals

Tissue-paper fairies

Materials
- Tissue paper in various colours
- Sewing thread in different colours
- Unspun wool or cotton wool
- Thick wire or cane for the hoop

2.5 *Tissue-paper fairies*

On a sheet of blank paper draw a circle with a radius of about 7 cm (2³/4 in). Then draw the wings (Figure 2.6). Cut out the two drawings.

Lay the cut-out patterns of the fairy and the wings on a sheet of tissue paper and cut out the two shapes. Using the patterns cut out the desired number of fairies.

Make a little ball of the unspun wool or cotton wool about the size of the tip of your little finger. Lay the ball in the middle of the round piece of tissue paper, fold one half over and make sure that the ball stays well in the middle to make the head. Tie a piece of similar coloured sewing-thread round the neck.

See which side is the best and make it the front. If the knot in the thread lands unexpectedly to the front, tie another knot at the back. Make sure that both ends of the thread are still long enough.

With these ends tie the wings firmly on to the middle of the back. Pull in the threads tight so that the wings don't wobble. Cut off the ends of the threads.

Take a fresh thread of the same colour and push it through the neck of the elf with a needle so that a thread comes out on each side of the head. Tie both threads about 4 cm (1¹/2 in) above the head.

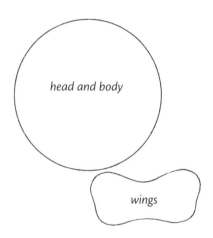

2.6 *Pattern for paper fairies*

Cut off one of the threads and use the other to hang the fairy up. You can now add a drape of tissue paper for a cloak.

Make a hoop of wire or piece of cane, wind coloured tissue paper around it and hang the fairies from it.

Tissue-paper butterflies

2.7 Tissue-paper butterflies

Materials

- ✪ Tissue paper in various colours
- ✪ Wooden skewer
- ✪ Poster paints
- ✪ Modelling wax (such as Stockmar)
- ✪ Thin wire
- ✪ Glue

For each butterfly select three different colours of paper. Cut out a sheet 8 × 9 cm (3 × 3^1/$_2$ in) and fold it in two so that you get the size 8 × 4.5 cm (3 × 1^3/4 in). Draw half a butterfly shape, with the body against the fold. Cut this out. Repeat this with the other two sheets.

Make the second set of wings slightly smaller (Figure 2.7). Draw the outline onto the second sheet of paper and cut the wings out, as described above. Repeat this with the third set of wings.

Stick the wings together in the fold with a little bit of glue. Make the butterfly's spots out of scraps of tissue paper and stick them on.

Take a wooden skewer and paint it. Fold a piece of thin wire in two. Twist the doubled end round the end of the skewer and cover the join with a blob of brown modelling wax. If necessary you can cut the ends of the wire to the right length and press little blobs of wax on to the two ends to form antennae.

Finally stick the wings firmly on to the skewer. Put the butterfly into a pot with flowers.

Paper doves

2.9 Dove mobile

1. On the cardboard first draw the head, body and tail of the dove, following the basic pattern in Figure 2.8. You can draw them bigger if you prefer. Cut them out and either cut out or draw on the eye. Make a slot in the middle of the body to take the wings.

2. For the wings take a piece of tissue paper or tracing paper 12 × 8 cm (4³/4 × 3¹/4 in). Mark twelve equal divisions along the long side, and fold the paper in concertina fashion twelve times.

3. Push the folded-up strip through the slot in the dove's body. Fold the two ends upwards and stick them together with a little bit of glue.

Insert a thread (using a needle) through the bird's feathers to hang it up. Figure 2.9 shows a mobile with twelve doves.

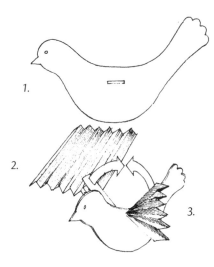

2.8 Making paper doves

Drying flowers and leaves

Throughout the year you can find various flowers to dry, for instance, roses, thistles, daisies and so on. Hang them in a dark, dry place by the stalk. Don't leave them in a vase until they have almost died; hang them up well before they start to wilt.

Leaf and flower press

Materials

- 2 plywood boards 20 × 20 cm (8 × 8 in) and 8 mm ($^3/_8$ in) thick
- 6–8 pieces of corrugated cardboard 20 × 20 cm (8 × 8 in)
- Sheets of tissue paper 20 × 20 cm (8 × 8 in)
- 4 bolts, 4–6 cm (2 in) long, 6 mm ($^1/_4$ in) diameter (No 14), with wing-nuts and washers

Sandpaper the plywood boards. Draw on the two diagonals to find the right place to make the holes, which should be about 2–3 cm (1 in) from the corners (Figure 2.10).

Press the bolts through the holes of one of the boards, hammering them in tight if necessary. Cut off the corners of the corrugated cardboard and the tissue papers so that they fit inside the bolts of the boards. Lay a few sheets of tissue paper between each layer of cardboard.

Lay the other board on top, fit the washers and tighten the nuts.

You can decorate the wooden boards of the flower press with crayons or paint.

To dry and press flowers and leaves, lay them carefully between two sheets of tissue paper, ensuring that any special features are preserved.

If any parts of the flower are too thick, such as a root, a stalk, a twig or the beginning of the fruit, carefully cut them away with a sharp knife, or cut the stalk in half.

Place the flower in the centre of the press, between the tissue and carboard and tighten the bolts. The flowers should be kept in the press for a few weeks in order to dry out thoroughly.

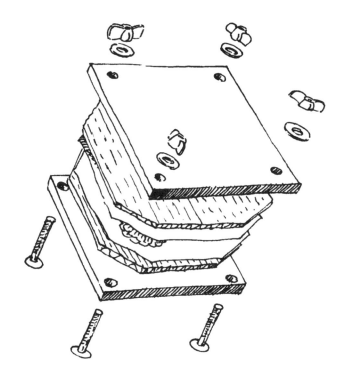

2.10 Making a flower press

Straw plaiting

From the time when people first grew grain, after the harvest had been gathered in, harvesters would make a symbol from the last sheaf of corn, which was then offered to the gods as thanksgiving for an abundant harvest and as a prayer for a new fruitful year. For example, in ancient Egypt straw was made into a doll, the *grain-mother*.

Through the centuries the form of this grain-mother or straw doll changed, and so with the coming of Christianity there came the harvest cross, which at the end of the harvest was carried to church (Figure 2.22). Right up to the beginning of this century many plaited symbols were made in England and other places in Europe, including those known as 'corn dollies'.

With combine harvesters, which thresh the corn and bale the straw at the same time, the custom of making a doll from the last sheaf has lapsed, and with it the skill of plaiting straw has also vanished. Some straw decorations described here are based on traditional motifs, others are new designs.

Materials
- Garden clippers or old scissors (for cutting straw)
- Sharp pointed scissors (for finishing off)
- Kitchen knife (for removing leaves from the stem)
- Thin string or strong thread (button thread) in natural colours
- Thick needles
- Tape measure

The length of the plait and the number of stems required is given as a guide for every pattern. Obviously, this can be varied.

For making decorations from straw and ears of corn, wheat or rye ears work best. Wheat straw is generally the easiest to use as it is fairly pliant.

Depending on the weather, harvesting takes place in July or August. Ask the farmer for straw or whole ears just before the corn is cut. See that the corn is not too near a road, which can make the grain rather grey and dirty.

Sometimes you can find some ears still standing along the edge of the cornfield after the cutting, or the harvester has left some cut corn which has not been threshed. For convenience this will be called 'waste straw'. Wind and rain will often rob it of its golden-yellow lustre leaving it a greenish colour. Even though the stalks are often broken and flattened they are still usable. The decorations in Figures 2.14, 2.15 and 2.18 are made of waste straw. Finally of course you can grow your own corn in a sunny patch of your garden. The colour of the ears is partly determined by the composition of the soil on which it grows. Soil containing iron can give a reddish-brown ear.

You don't always need stalks with ears, which can be cut off at the first nodule. If, however, the *whole stalk* is required see that the ear stands up nicely.

Wheat with its chaff-husks has a beautiful form.

Barley ears have grains in two rows which give a characteristic effect.

The light, airy *oat* is generally used only for decoration.

Stalks

The stalk consists of a long stem with nodules at regular intervals. Out of these nodules grow long narrow leaves which are wrapped round the stalk. The stalk is thicker at the bottom than up at the ear, becoming thinner at each nodule.

The further apart the nodules, the better the stalk is suited for plaiting, because the nodules are tough and cannot be bent easily. If the stalks are very thick at the bottom and very thin at the top, it is best to use only the middle part of the stalk, because the lower part is then often too hard to plait and the top looks too thin.

Stalks are best stored by binding them together with an elastic band and hanging the bunch upside down (reducing the chance of breaking the ears).

The length of the stalks depends on the type of grain, where it grows, the humidity and the temperature in springtime. The length you need is determined by the kind of work you are doing.

2.11 Cereal bouquet

Cereal bouquet

Materials

- Basket
- Oasis (florist's flower block)
- Knife
- Cereals: oat, wheat, rye and barley

1. Cut out a good piece of oasis measured so that it fits neatly into the basket, leaving about 1.5–2 cm (3/4 in) above the rim (Figure 2.12, page 64).

2. Imagine or lightly draw a triangle *A1–A2–A3* on to the surface of the oasis. Push three ears of the same kind of cereal obliquely into the rim of the oasis below each point.

3. Now imagine or lightly draw a second triangle *B1–B2–B3*, and insert an ear of another kind into the oasis below each of these points. Repeat this with a third triangle, *C1–C2–C3*. Make sure that all the ears are of the same length so that the basket, when made up, will be nice and round.

Push a good ear of wheat or rye into the centre of the oasis. You can insert another three ears obliquely a little away from the centre of the oasis.

4. Fill the whole piece of oasis *lightly* with oat ears 8–10 cm (3–4 in) high. This grain is softer and hides the oasis.

Begin inserting the remaining ears towards the middle, working from below up and going round all the time. Ears that are hanging down should of course be facing outwards.

Preparing to plait

Before stalks can be worked they must be peeled, that is to say the long thin leaves which often lie closely around the stalk must be removed. This is best done by running a potato peeler down the stalk from top to bottom. This must be done carefully otherwise the stalk can break at the nodules (Figure 2.13). Make sure that the leaves are completely removed round the nodules.

By nature, dry stalks are stiff and not pliable, so before plaiting they must be soaked. Lay them in a bath or tub with warm water for an hour, weighing them down with a bowl or plate so that they lie well covered with water (Figure 2.14). Only freshly cut stalks are still pliant enough to be plaited without being soaked.

Don't leave the stalks in the water for too long, as this will affect their quality adversely. So don't soak any more than you require for plaiting. You will need some practice before being able to judge how much straw you will need for any particular article. Depending on the thickness and tightness of the plait, it will be 50–60% of the length of the flat straws, so for each plait you will need two or three times its length in straw.

2.12 Making the bouquet

2.13 Trimming stalks

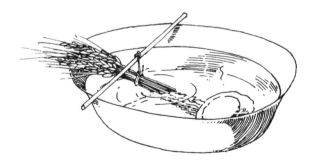

2.14 Soaking stalks

Straw heart

Materials
- Waste straw
- Length: c. 66 cm (26 in)

2.15 Straw hearts

Use stems without ears. Take them out of the water, cutting off any bits that are too thin and any nodules at the end of the stalks. Although there are various methods of plaiting only the simplest with three straws will be used in this book.

For the straw hearts in Figure 2.15 begin with twelve or fifteen stalks depending on their thickness. As stalks are thinner at the top, turn some round so that the thickness of the bundle remains even.

1. To get as tight a plait as possible tie the end of the bundle of straws firmly together with string (Figure 2.16, page 66).

2. For this a clove-hitch is a handy knot as it can be drawn tight immediately. Then tie an extra knot if necessary. In order to plait tightly tie the other end of the string to something.

3. For plaiting you can use a plaiting board, which is a board about 25 × 80 cm (10 × 32 in) with four nails driven in at one end. As the plaiting proceeds the string can be wound round the nails so that the actual point of plaiting remains at the same distance from your body.

Now follow the steps in Figure 2.17.

1. Divide the bundle of straw into three equal parts.

2. First the bundle of straws furthest to the right C is brought over the bundle in the middle B.

3. Then bring the left-hand bundle A over bundle C, which has now become the middle bundle.

4. Then bring the right-hand bundle over the middle one, and so on.

It is important to keep an angle of 90° between the bundles. This gives the best plaiting result.

Often the straw will still be stiff even though they have been soaked. Press the stems together between your thumb and forefinger before the bundle is plaited. If the straw becomes very dry during plaiting, lay the plait back into the water for 5–10 minutes. Tie the loose end of the plait to prevent it coming apart.

Adding new stems

One of the bundles may come to an end before the plait is finished. Stages 5 and 6 in Figure 2.17 show how to proceed.

5. Lay one or more straws on the remains of the bundle.

6. Then fold one of the other bundles over it and continue plaiting.

Obviously you will have a problem if all the bundles come to an end at the same time. To avoid this make sure at the beginning that the bundles are of different lengths. Once the plait is finished, cut off all bits of straw that stick out.

Finishing

7. Once the desired length of plaiting has been achieved, tie up the three bundles together. Cut off any excess straw, smooth the wet plait into the required shape and sew it up with a needle and thread (Figure 2.17).

The plait will require about 24 hours to dry completely. While it is drying lay something heavy on it (such as a board) to keep it nice and flat. After drying, trim the ends.

For decorating and making up plaits see page 92.

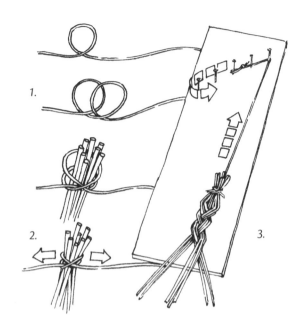

2.16 Preparing to plait

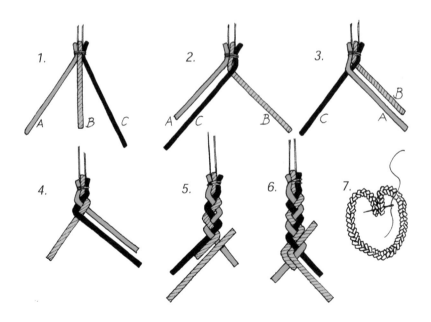

2.17 Plaiting straw

Double straw heart

Materials
✪ Waste straw
✪ Red ribbon
✪ Length: inside heart c. 52 cm (20$^{1}/_{2}$ in);
   outside heart c. 70 cm (27$^{1}/_{2}$ in)

2.18 Double straw heart

The double straw heart is a variation of the single heart. The method is the same, only the finishing off is different because the hearts need to be fixed together.

Make two plaits of different lengths.

1. Fold the longer plait over in the middle and sew up the fold with a few stitches (Figure 2.19).

2. Fold the shorter one over in the middle round the first plait and sew it a bit lower down on to the first plait.

3. Now bend the outside (shortest) plait-ends down to make a heart shape and sew the ends together with a few stitches.

4. Then bend the long inside plait-end round it and sew the ends on to the other heart firmly.

5. After drying, cut off the inside end of the joined hearts and trim the bottom joint neatly. Hang the hearts up with red ribbon or red wool.

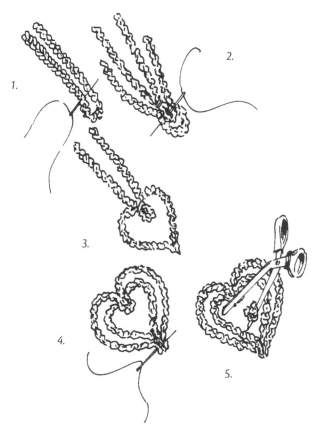

2.19 Tying a double heart

Straw wreath

Materials
- Wheat or rye straw
- Length: 70–80 cm (28–32 in)

2.20 Straw wreath

With the straw heart the ends were sewn together so that the plaiting was done side-on. With a wreath (Figure 2.20) you see the plaiting head-on and the two ends are laid one over the other. Here a tied-up bundle of straws would not look good at the beginning, so this plaiting is begun in a different way (Figure 2.21).

1. Take a bunch of wet stalks (some of which are head to tail to make it even) which is only half as thick as necessary. Separate into three bundles, making sure they are of different lengths.

2. Bend them double. Make sure the bundles have different lengths, so that when they are plaited they don't all come to an end together.

For the rest the plaiting is the same as that of the straw heart (Figure 2.17). When the plaiting is finished, tie off the ends, and then sew them together tightly.

Dry this plait under weight to prevent the wreath from warping.

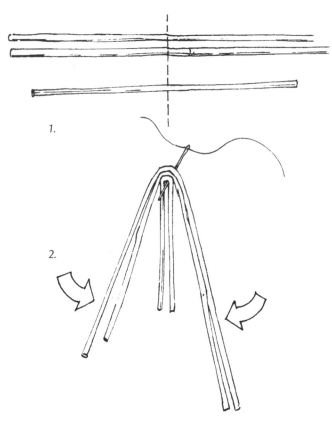

2.21 Preparing to plait

Harvest-cross wreath

Materials
- ✪ Wheat or rye straw for plaiting
- ✪ Barley with grains in two rows for the wreath of ears
- ✪ Oat and wheat with chaff husks for decoration
- ✪ Circumference: c. 62 cm (24 in); length of cross: 20 cm (8 in)

2.22 Harvest-cross wreath

For plaiting the wreath (Figure 2.22) you'll need fifteen stalks.

Plait in the same way as the straw wreath, but add a barley ear (with its two rows of grain) each time on one side during the plaiting (Figure 2.23). Make sure that the ear sticks out nicely and cannot turn. The barley straw is gripped between the other stems.

If the bundle becomes too thick and the plaiting uneven, cut off the barley stalks after a few folds. Barley stems are quite thin so it may be necessary to strengthen them here and there with thin wire.

Make the cross by sewing one short plait on top of another.

It is best to sew the cross on to the circle after drying. In the picture the plaiting is decorated with a round oat posy, accentuating the form of the plait work.

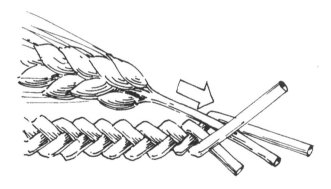

2.23 Adding ears

Sun made of ears

Materials
- ✪ Stalks of the same thickness
- ✪ 12 wheat ears with husks
- ✪ Strong thread

Cut soaked stalks into twelve equal lengths of 10 cm (4 in) and flatten them with an iron.

Lay six straws one on top of the other as shown in Figure 2.25. The first and last straw form a cross enclosing the other straws.

The thread which binds the crosses together is passed from behind and goes over the last straw, under the next one, and so on. In this way a 12-pointed star is produced.

With the remaining straws make a second star with twelve points, place one star on top of the other. Weave a thread through them, tie them together and cut off the surplus threads.

Cut every second ray of the star 3 cm (1¹/4 in) from the centre, and cut the remaining long rays into points (Figure 2.26).

Take the twelve wheat ears and cut off the stalks leaving only a stem of about 1 cm (¹/2 in). Dab a bit of glue on it. Now take the rays, which have been ironed flat and cut short, between your thumb and forefinger and one by one squeeze them open and insert the stem of the ear into them.

Hang up your sun!

Variation

In the sun in Figure 2.24, 24 ears are used instead of twelve with alternately a larger and smaller ear.

2.24 Sun with 24 ears

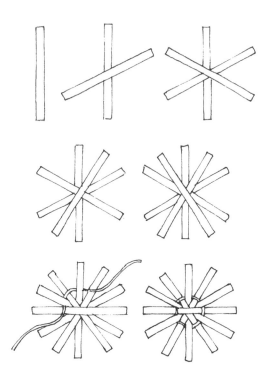

2.25 Making the sun

2.26 Sun made of ears

Welsh Corn dolly

2.27 Welsh corn dolly

Materials
- ☼ Wheat stems with ears
- ☼ Length: 35 cm (14 in)

This is a very decorative plait (Figure 2.27) which needs some practice to make it really beautifully. Practise with straws that are not very good quality.

1. Following the diagrams in Figure 2.28, tie three wet wheat straws with ears (A, B and C) together just below the ears and fan them out. Now add two new straws D and E.

2. The new straws are kept in place by bending straws A and C round them.

3. The basic technique is shown clearly: straw B weaves alternately under and over (under E, over A, under D and over C). Always begin by going under and finish by going over the last straw.

4. and 5. After every three folds at the edge of the plait add a new straw with the ear protruding. Look carefully at the Figure to see how the new straws are added ensuring an even pattern.

You can make the plait as long as you like. The corn dolly in Figure 2.27 is made from 25 straws with ears and is 35 cm (14 in) long.

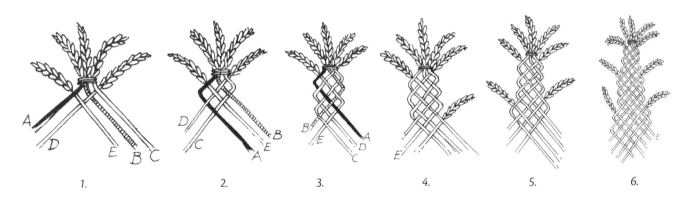

2.28 Making a Welsh corn dolly

Four-straw plaited decoration

Four-straw plaiting results in a three-dimensional 'rope', rather than a flat braid (Figure 2.29).

1. Tie four wet stalks (*A, B, C* and *D*) together as shown in Figure 2.30 — just below the ears with strong thread. Then spread them out at right angles.

2. Now fold straw *A* towards *B* and straw *B* to where *A* was.

3. Then fold straw *C* to *D* and straw *D* to where *C* was.

Begin again with *A* and *B* and then with *C* and *D*. Continue in this way until the plait is about 18 cm (7 in) long, and then tie the four stems together so that the plaiting does not come apart. Let the unplaited straws hang for now; they should be about 20 cm (8 in) long.

Make another plait with four fresh stems. Tie the two plaits together just below the ears. Shape them into a heart by tying the other ends together, leaving the unplaited stalks pointing down (Figure 2.29).

Tie the unplaited straws with the ears together and cut them off obliquely so they tuck into the base of the heart. Arrange the ears nicely and, if you want to, add a coloured ribbon.

2.29 Four-straw plaited decoration

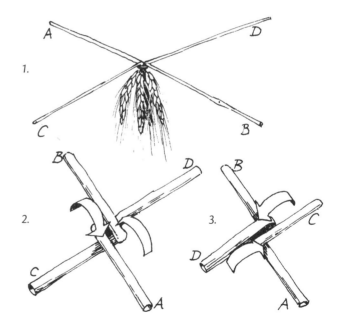

2.30 Four-straw plaiting

Lengthening stalks

When plaiting with single stems you cannot add new pieces as described earlier (page 66), as it would cause a break in the plaiting.

Usually the end of the straw is thick. If there is a nodule at the end, cut it off.

Take a thinner stalk and insert it into the opening of the old one, gently pushing it as far as it will go. Don't push too hard, or you will split the outside straw.

Take care when bending the lengthened straw.

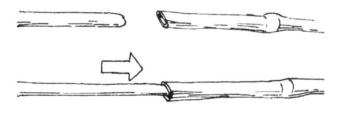

2.31 Lengthening stems

Straw plaiting with spirals

Spiral plaiting preparation

Materials
- ✪ Long thin stems
- ✪ Thread

This kind of plaiting, which originates in England, has various forms with innumerable variations. It is exacting work, which must be done with care and patience to ensure even plaiting. Don't be tempted to work too quickly, for the plaiting will become loose and untidy and you will only notice when it's too late to correct.

Use thin pliant straw because it has to be completely folded over. The upper part of the stalks are best. If a stalk has too many nodules, when sharply bent it can break or the nodules protrude and spoil the regular shape of the spiral.

While plaiting, keep a look out for nodules approaching. If necessary cut the straw before the nodule and lengthen it as just described (Figure 2.31). Take care that the plaiting remains taut while you are extending the straw.

While you are working you can widen or reduce the plait, or keep the same width.

Spiral plaiting is always three-dimensional. The technique remains the same whether you plait with three, four or more corners according to the number of straws used.

Spiral plaiting with padding

The models in this book have four corners. For this five stalks are required for plaiting. Plaiting with padding is easier because the padding gives support during plaiting. The plaiting forms a kind of long tube and so is less bendable than plaiting without padding, which is described later.

Take a bundle of stalks, not necessarily all with ears, the minimum number being ten. The thickness of the plait will be affected by the number of stems you use. For the decoration on the left of Figure 2.32, ten straws with ears are used.

Tie up the straws together just below the ears (Figure 2.33). Turn the straws upside down so that the ears are pointing down and the stalks up.

1. Bend five stalks on the outside of the bundle so that they are pointing out horizontally in four directions. The remaining straws form the padding. Work straw *E* under *D* and then back over *D* so that it comes next to straw *A*.

2. Then move the plait a quarter-turn anticlockwise so that now straws *A* and *E* are pointing to the right. Now work straw *A* under and over *E* to come next to *B*. Repeat this procedure until the plait has nearly reached the desired length and the straws have become quite short.

3. Now cut the padding off and plait one or two more rows making the plait thinner to finish.

4. Then tie the five stalks at the top of the plait together.

Finally cut off the tied straws evenly and if desired adorn the plait with a coloured bow. If the ears make too big a bunch, cut a few off.

2.32 Spiral-plaited decorations

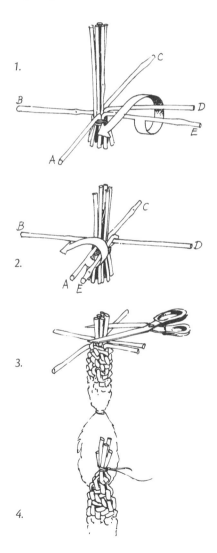

2.33 Spiral plaiting

Hollow spiral plaiting

Once you have learned to plait with padding you can try making hollow spiral plaiting. Take special care that the plait remains taut. The principle has already been described but this kind of plaiting allows the spiral form to become wider or narrower.

Bringing straw E next to A (Figure 2.33, step 1), but leaving a little gap before laying straw A over E, allows the plait to become wider as shown in the decoration on the right of Figure 2.32.

If E lies on top of A the plait will retain the same width. If E lies to the left of A then the plait will become narrower again.

Figure 2.34 shows a mobile of straw spirals of different sizes. Of course you can also use stems with ears if you like. The hangers of the mobile are made with copper wire, and the spirals are hung with red wool to add a bit of colour.

Variation: cup-shaped plaiting

To make a spiral plait that is open at the bottom, finish it off at the desired length and leave it open instead of decreasing it to a point.

To finishing it off at the last row, secure each straw with thread to the straw beside it. Then cut off the bits of straw sticking out.

2.34 Straw-spiral mobile

Straw dolls and animals

Straw billy goat (Yule-buck)

2.35 *Straw billy goat*

This straw billy goat (or Yule-buck) comes from Sweden (Figure 2.35). The number and the length of straws given are only a guide and can be varied.

Wet straw is more pliant and it can be dried in its bent form. For the goat described here the straw has to be bent quite considerably, so it helps to use wire to hold the straw in shape.

Begin with the horns (Figure 2.36, page 78). For these select two lots of three straws which aren't too thick and have a long stem without nodules.

1. Insert a very thin wire into at least two of the three straws, tie the three straws together and make a plait of about 15 cm (6 in).

2. Roll up the plait and secure it, but don't cut off the unplaited ends. Because of the wire inside the straw, the horns will remain in the required shape. Repeat for the second horn.

Then take 20–25 of the 45 cm (18 in) straws for the goat's head, neck and body. Lay the straws alternately head to tail so that the thin ends are evenly distributed. Insert the copper wire into two straws. If there is a nodule in the straw push the copper wire in from both ends up to the nodule.

3. Now tie the bundle together at one end (clove-hitch with a few extra knots, Figure 2.16).

4. Fold it over about 3–4 cm (1 1/2 in) from the end. Then insert the horns into the bundle (the goat's neck) and secure.

Now fill the bundle by inserting a further five to eight stalks.

5. Fold over the bundle once more to make the body and this can now be secured. The wire will hold the bundle of straws in the required shape.

6. For the legs take two lots of fifteen straws about 30 cm (12 in) long. Again insert copper wire into two straws so that the bundle will stand in the right shape. Tie up the forelegs in two places and now make the second bundle similarly.

7. Fold both bundles to make them part of the goat's body and secure behind the forelegs, passing the thread a couple of times round the body before tying. Add a few straws if the body is too thin. Now fold the leg bundles over to make the hind legs and tie them up in two places.

8. From the unfinished end of the head-and-body piece select six stalks to plait into a tail after inserting two thin wires. Then trim the remaining stalks. Roll up the plaited tail and trim the legs.

Bend the horns into a good shape and stick a little bundle of oat-heads or grasses as a billy goat's gruff below the head in the neck. Now go over all the knots and cut off the loose threads, if necessary putting a touch of glue on the ends.

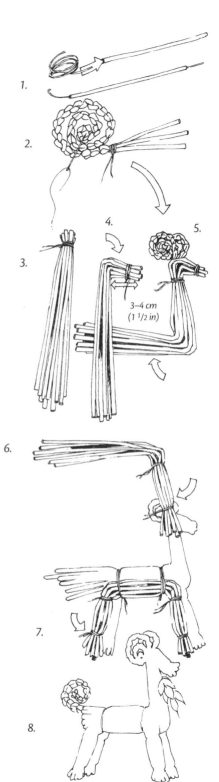

2.36 Making the billy goat

Straw cockerel

Materials
- ✪ Straw
- ✪ Oat stems or dried grasses
- ✪ Thin wire
- ✪ Copper wire
- ✪ Thread in various colours

1. Using damp straw make two plaits, each with three stems (Figure 2.38, page 80). The plait should be about 6–7 cm (2^1/2 in) long, with loose straw at both ends extending another 3 cm (1^1/4 in).

2. Tie each plait into a loop. They make the gills of the cockerel.

For the cockerel's comb make three plaits of equal length, but plait only the middle of the straws, leaving about 20 cm (8 in) at each end of the plait. Tie these plaits into loops.

For the head-and-body piece you need fifteen straws about 35 cm (14 in) long. The method is roughly the same as that for the billy goat. When tying the head tie in the plaited comb (Figure 2.38, step 7) and tie the plaited gills into the neck at the same time.

For the legs you will need about twelve stalks approximately 22 cm (9 in) long. Try to select stems without nodules. Insert thin wire into three straws and lay these aside. Insert the thicker copper wire into two other straws.

Legs and claws

Make the toes at the ends of the straws. Because they tend to split when bent over, exposing the wire inside, the ends are finished off with a whipping, which is done as follows (Figure 2.38, steps 3–6).

2.37 Straw cockerel

3. Place one of the straws (which were laid aside) with wire in it and one plain straw together. Lay a loop of thread over the end of the straw.

4. Pass the long end of the thread round the loop and round both straws.

5. Now wind the thread tightly round the loop and both straws until the binding is about 8–10 mm (3/8 in) wide. Push end A through the loop and pull the thread tight.

6. By pulling *B* the loop will disappear below the binding. Cut off the visible end *A*, pull it right under the binding and cut off end *B*.

Repeat this whipping at the other end of the two straws, and then make two more bundles of two straws tied at each end. You now have three lengths of double straw (one plain and one with wire) with each end whipped.

Put these six stalks and the remaining six together into a bundle of twelve and tie the bundle at each end about 5 mm (¼ in) from the whippings.

Bend the bundle round to make a U. Insert it into the body of the cockerel and tie it in.

Tail

Now bend the tail up from the body. The wire in the straws will ensure that they maintain their shape. Because the rest will dry into shape tie up the tail into one bundle and allow the cockerel to dry.

When the cockerel is dry cut the tie, and the straws of the tail should fan out. They may need smoothing down here and there.

7. Cut the tail straws one by one to different lengths (Figure 2.38). For the tail wild oats were used which grow at the edge of fields and have no seeds (the seeds would make the tail too heavy). Alternatively use grasses.

Apply a little glue to the ends of the oat stalks or grasses inserted into the tail. Continue with this until you have an ample tail.

Now bend the whipped claws into the right shape (two to the front, and one to the back) and cut off the surplus straw at the ankle. If you leave the thick copper wire in place you can make a stand for the cockerel by inserting the wire into two holes in a piece of bark or wood.

To finish off you can of course use a spray with some watercolour paint to give the oats or grasses some colour.

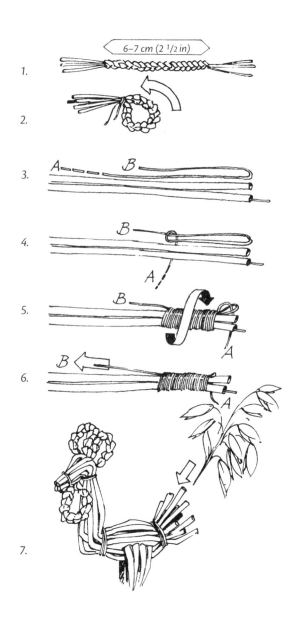

2.38 *Making the cockerel*

2.39 Straw dolls

Plaited straw dolls

Materials
- ✪ 9–12 long stems of straw
- ✪ Thread in various colours

Depending on the thickness of the stems, take nine to twelve straws for plaiting. Tie them together 10 cm (4 in) from the end (Figure 2.40).

1. Plait the long end of the straws to a length of about 12 cm (4 1/2 in). Tie up the plait and fold it double.

2. About 2 cm (3/4–1 in) from the fold, tie both parts of the plait together with button thread to make the neck. The button thread should be strong enough to make the neck narrower than the head.

Now plait the arms. In Figure 2.39 you can see two methods of plaiting: the women have arms of the usual plait and the men have four-straw plaited arms (Figure 2.30). With the women's arms you can see the difference between thick and thin straws.

Make the arms 10 cm (4 in) long and tie them up well at both sides. Place the arms between the two ends of the large plait directly below the neck.

3. Now tie up the waist with button thread at the place where the two ends of the plait are tied together (Figure 2.40).

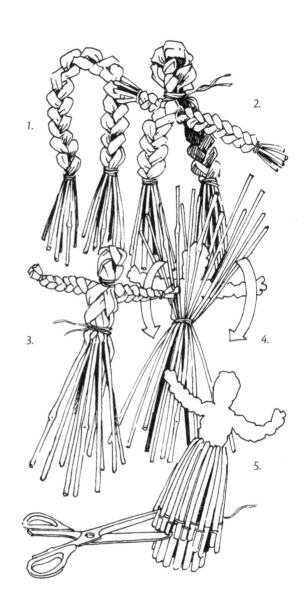

2.40 Making straw dolls

4. The lower body of the *woman* consists of unplaited straws about 7 cm (3 in) long. In its present form it is still too thin, so lay some bits of straw — preferably without nodules — round the waist. Hold them tight with one hand and tie these straws with the other hand firmly to the waist.

5. Now fold down the stems that are sticking up at the waist. Because these stems which form the skirt tend not to stay in place, tie them together loosely from under the skirt.

Lay the doll in water for a few minutes. Allow the doll to dry and then release the tie; the straws should then nearly always stay down.

In Figure 2.39 one of the women has an apron because the straws which were pointing up have been folded down, cut off shorter and tied down with a coloured thread.

For the *man*, divide the unplaited straws of the lower body in two after tying up the waist, plait the two halves into legs and tie them at the ends.

While it is easy to get women to stand, with men it is more difficult. It should be possible if the feet are trimmed properly. If you like you can plait copper wire into the two legs, leaving a bit protruding, which you can insert into a bark or wooden base.

For the *baby* (held by the central doll), use some leftover stems, fold them into two and tie them up. Of course the body can also be plaited and you can clothe the dolls with little bits of cloth or dried leaves.

The *basket* is made from a plait of three ears. The plaits are sewn together with thread to make a basket. Bigger baskets and boxes can be made in the same way by using more stems.

Corn-husk dolls

Corn (maize) husks were used by Native Americans to make baskets, rugs and toys. The colonists of the New World learned their skills and passed these back to Europe, where particularly the Czechs are known for their meticulously crafted dolls.

The leaf-sheaths surrounding the corn cob make up the basic material for these dolls. If you cannot buy corn cobs with covering leaves, find a farmer who grows maize and ask him for a few cobs.

Preparing the leaves

The husks are brittle, so the cobs must be peeled carefully. Cut the husks round the stalk (Figure 2.41). Remove the fuzzy silks carefully from the top of the cob, and dry them well in the sun (if they are not quite dry they can go mouldy). They will come in handy to use as hair.

The fine, thin leaves of the cob are best dried and flattened in a flower press or a telephone book with a weight on it (if they are dried in the sun they will curl). If the leaves have a yellowish green colour after being dried, lay them out in the sun and the greenish colour will be bleached away.

Dry the rough, brittle husks of the cob itself in the sun to use as stuffing.

The dried leaves look and can be cut like paper. They are fun to work with, so try to lay them carefully in a good store.

Making the doll

Materials

- ✪ Dried leaf-sheaths of corn cob (maize)
- ✪ Dried corn silks
- ✪ Balls of cotton wool, cork or polystyrene with a diameter of 8–24 mm (3/8–1 in)
- ✪ Cotton wool
- ✪ Very thin wire
- ✪ Copper wire 0.8 mm (20 gauge)
- ✪ Buttonhole thread in suitable colours
- ✪ Glue
- ✪ Large needle or awl
- ✪ Scissors

Although the husks are first dried they can generally only be worked when they are moistened to make them pliant. Dry husks tend to break.

Lay a few leaves in a basin of lukewarm water for 5 minutes. Note that wet husks expand and shrink again when they are drying.

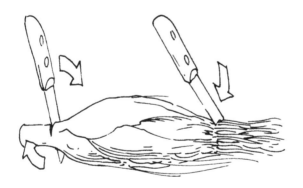

2.41 Preparing husks

Head

Begin with the head. You need a little ball as padding which can be made of cotton wool, cork or polystyrene, or even a round wooden bead.

If none of these is available cut up a dry husk into strips about 5 mm (1/4 in) as in Figure 2.42. Cut along the width (across the veins).

Make a little ball out of these strips. Stick the ends of the strips together with glue. The biggest dolls shown here have a head with a diameter of about 25 mm (1 in).

1. With a strong needle or an awl make a hole through the ball and push a piece of wire right through (Figure 2.43).

2. Twist the ends together. The wire must not be too short as it will be needed to strengthen the body.

3. Select a good thin (but not too wide) wet leaf. Put the ball in the middle and wrap one side of the leaf over the ball. Make sure that the wire passes from one ear past the chin to the other ear.

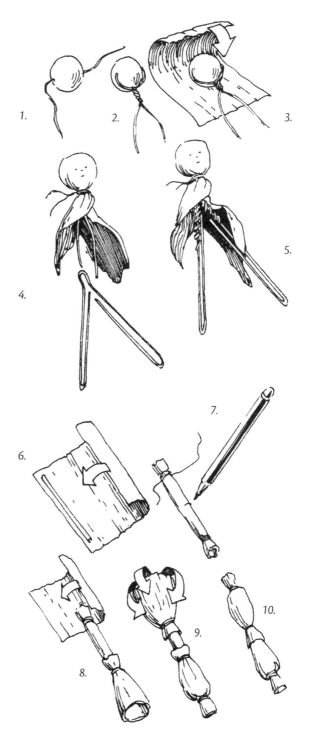

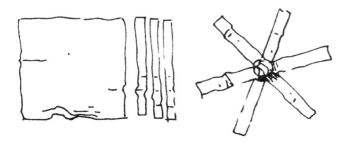

2.42 Head made from husks

2.43 Making the head and arms

4. Now wrap the leaf round the ball with as few folds as possible, keeping the folds to one side, which will become the back of the head. With buttonhole thread wrap the leaf as tightly as possible round the neck and secure. To make a neck wind the thread four or five times round the neck and secure again. The rest of the maize leaf is left to hang. Take a copper wire about 30 cm (12 in) long. Fold it as shown to make the body and legs (Figure 2.43).

5. Wind the thin wire from the head around the copper leg wires.

Arms

For the doll's arms take a piece of copper wire (or thin wires twisted together) about 10 cm (4 in) long.

6. Wrap a piece of maize leaf round the wire (Figure 2.43). The leaf should stick out about 1 cm ($^1/_2$ in) at each end and should be about 7–8 cm (3 in) long depending on the thickness of the leaf (a thin leaf needs to be wrapped more times round otherwise the arms look too thin).

7. Tie the rolled-up leaf just below each end of the wire. Mark the middle of the arms with a pen.

8. Give the arms sleeves: the women half or three-quarter sleeves; the men long sleeves. For this use a maize leaf 6 × 6 cm ($2^1/_2$ × $2^1/_2$ in). The sleeves are gathered and tied to the arms.

9. Then turn them outside in.

10. Secure the sleeves in the middle of the arms. If the sleeves don't puff out, fill them with some leftover husks.

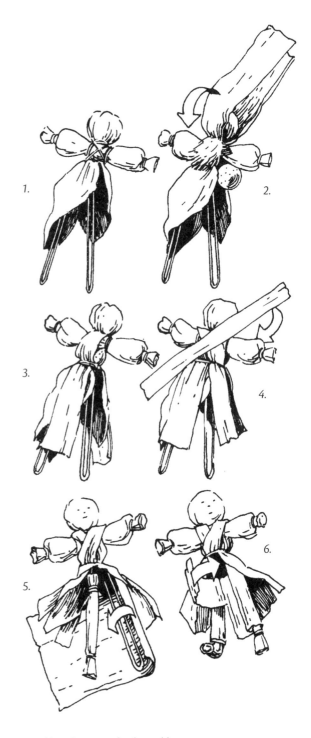

2.44 Making the upper body and legs

Upper body

1. Following Figure 2.44, secure the arms to the head, making sure that a bit of the neck still shows. Choose the side of the head with the least folds to make into the face. Fix the arms to the back of the neck by criss-crossing some thread round them and securing.

2. Now fill the body and the back. For this tie two narrow husks (about 3 cm, 1¹/₄ in wide) to the middle of the neck immediately above the arms. Fill the back where the arms are secured with a little ball of cotton wool.

For the stomach take half a ball of cotton wool or cork of the same size as the head.

3. Fold the strips of tied-on maize leaf over the cotton wool and tie them at the waist with thread.

4. To finish off the shoulders cut a few husk strips about 10–15 mm (¹/₂ in) wide. Lay one of the strips obliquely from the left shoulder to the right side of the waist and secure there. Repeat for the other side. Repeat this again if the side of the upper body is not quite covered. Finally do this once more, fastening the strips more loosely round the upper body, so that when they dry and shrink they don't become tight. These last strips form the blouse.

2.45 Corn-husk dolls

2.46 Dolls with coloured aprons

Lower body (man)

5. Make legs and trousers (Figure 2.44). For this the two ends of the wire are wrapped separately with husks and tied at the top and bottom. Then bend the ends of the legs to make feet. Now make the trousers by wrapping leaves round the legs until they are thick enough.

6. The last husk is cut and the top wound round the upper body. If necessary stick the husk with glue when it is dry.

To make baggier trousers, wrap a gathered leaf loosely round the leg and secure it only at the thigh.

Make knickerbockers in the same way as puffed sleeves, but first secure the husk at the ankle, then turn it inside out and secure it at the thigh.

You can cover all rough ends and loose bits by giving the doll a smock (Figure 2.45).

Lower body (woman)

The lower body of the women can be filled, or simply consist of a skirt and petticoat (Figure 2.47).

1. For a filled lower body you can take leftover husks. Cut them into strips, wet them and lay them out as a fan, placing the doll on its back in the middle.

2. Now secure the strips to the waist. Repeat this with the doll lying on its front.

3. Fold the husks above the waist down, and tie them together.

4. Select one or two good (damp) leaves and wrap the whole doll up in them, securing them at the waist, bending the arms up beside the head. Fold the top half of the leaf down and smooth it.

5. Trim the bottom of the skirt so that the doll can stand. With this filled skirt it is important that the husks inside are really dry to avoid their going mouldy. To dry the doll put it near a radiator for a few days.

2.47 Making skirts

If you are making a doll with an unfilled lower body, which has only a skirt and petticoat, then just follow the instructions for the last maize leaves. Take care that the skirt flounces out well and is firm so that the doll will stand.

The advantage of this skirt is that you can bend the doll's legs and she can sit or kneel. Make sure that the wire is not visible.

Finishing off

Once the dolls have been thoroughly dried, trim all the edges of the maize leaves and secure all the loose thread with glue.

The dolls can now be dressed with dry husks which can be cut and stuck on.

Use the curly silks for hair. They can be plaited if moistened.

Husks can be coloured by fabric dying or batik. However, it is very laborious, and we will not describe it further here.

The light tints of the skirts shown in Figure 2.46 were obtained by laying the leaves in a basin of concentrated watercolours for half an hour, then rinsing them in clean water. Dry them afterwards in a flower press.

You can colour the husks with a spray before cutting out the clothing. Alternatively colour the finished doll with a paintbrush and watercolours.

2.48 Baked Whitsun bird

Baked Whitsun bird

Make dough using the recipe on page 22. Divide the dough into eight portions.

Roll each portion into a long strip and tie a knot in it. Make a few cuts into the tail.

With a knife make a hole for the eye and one for the beak. You can put a raisin in for the eye and a nut for the beak.

3. Autumn

You can make lots of beautiful objects from things that are scattered on the ground in gardens, parks, grass verges or woods in late summer and autumn. Mostly they can be gathered without harming any trees or plants. For example: cereals and grasses, chestnuts (conkers), pine cones, fir cones, acorns, beechnuts, hazelnuts, hop cones, rosehips, hogweed blossom, honesty pennies, dried leaves, maple or sycamore seeds, feathers.

Keep the collection of materials in a dry place with plenty of air. Take care especially that chestnuts and acorns don't go mouldy (don't keep them in a plastic bag). You can store different kinds of cereals, grasses and tassels in tall glasses. For other materials simple cardboard trays are handy.

Cardboard storage tray

Materials
✪ Thick paper or thin card (letter, A4 or larger)

1. Fold the paper or card in half and half again, once along the long side and once on the short side (Figure 3.2).

2. Raise the long sides first, then raise one of the short sides, fold the corner inwards and glue it together.

3. Fold the overlapping piece to the short side inwards and stick it with a bit of glue. Do the same with the other short side and the tray is finished.

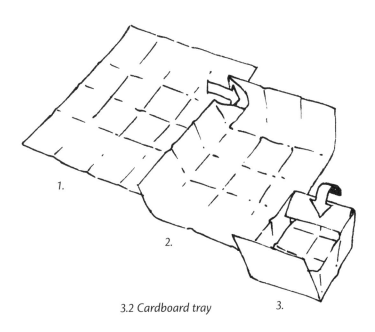

3.2 Cardboard tray

Opposite: 3.1 Harvest gathering

Harvest decorations

Mounting on wire

Materials
- ✪ Various harvest findings
- ✪ Thin wire (0.4 mm, 26 gauge)

To make a bouquet or posy use fine wire to bind together each separate item. Keep the stems as short as possible to avoid the posy becoming too thick.

1. Take a piece of wire about 15 cm (6 in) long, bend it double, making a loop with one end pointing down (Figure 3.3).

2. Take a stem and hold it tight between your thumb and forefinger so that the loop can be passed round it.

3. Let one end of the wire lie against the stalk and wind the other end three or four times tightly round them. Let the ends of the wire lie next to each other. It is possible to set several stalks together on to wire in this way. Make sure that the two loose ends of the wire are of about the same length, so that when the posy is finished they will give it enough support.

4. To attach wire to leaves or honesty pennies, push one end of the wire through the leaf a little bit above the lower edge and bend it carefully downwards.

5. Take the leaf between your thumb and forefinger and wind one end of the wire two or three times tightly round the other end, then bring it straight down.

6. To attach wire to pine cones, push a wire through the bottom row of scales near the stalk of a dry cone.

7. Twist one end of the wire a few times round the other.

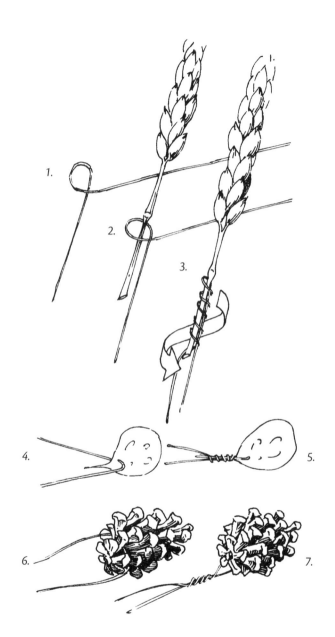

3.3 Mounting on wire

Making a posy

3.4 Harvest posy

Figure 3.5 shows the various stages in making a posy.

1. First choose the materials for your posy and set them on wire (Figure 3.3).

2. Begin with a long object such as an ear of corn. Then choose something to go with it. Hold both articles in one hand and, with the other, twist their wires round each other — enough to secure them firmly without thickening the posy.

3. Now take a leaf or a sprig of conifer, for example, and lay it over the wire of the first two materials. Twist the wire round this once, so that the wire does not show at the top.

In this way one thing after the other can be added. Look carefully at the posy from the front to see where the next piece should go, attach it firmly and don't adjust things that are already attached.

To conceal the wire stems attach one or more leaves to the posy and then bend them back over the wire. You may find an opening in the heart of the posy which can be filled with something round such as a pine cone, or a sprig of conifer.

Once the posy is finished, take a piece of wire out of the middle and twist this firmly round the other wires, cutting off the end at the required length with your wire clippers.

Tie up the posy firmly with a piece of wire — or with needle and thread — to a plaited wreath, a little piece of wood (Figure 3.4) or something similar.

1.   2.   3.

3.5 Making a posy

Decorated pine cone

Materials

- Large pine cone
- Modelling clay, diameter about 2.5 cm (1 in)
- Thin plastic (from a plastic bag)
- Ribbon
- Wire (approx. 0.7 mm, 21 gauge)
- Various harvest materials set on wire

For decorating a pine cone use suitable materials from a wood. When finished it can be hung up or laid down.

Pass a piece of wire through the scales near the stem (Figure 3.3, steps 6 and 7).

Place the lump of clay in the thin plastic (which helps to keep it firm) and attach it to the pine cone with the wire, together with a bow of ribbon. The lump of clay will come to sit more or less between the scales.

Cut off the wire ends as short as possible, bending back the sharp ends and sticking them into the lump of clay.

The pine cone can now be hung up, and the decorations (already set on wire) can be pushed into the lump of clay, keeping the wires short. If it is difficult to insert the materials prick some holes in the plastic with a large needle.

Pine-cone sun

Materials

- Pine cone
- Grasses, plant tassels (panicles), and so on
- Strong glue

Select a nice round pine cone and stick on all kinds of grasses and tassels (panicles) between the scales in a circle round it.

It is best to work layer by layer, looking all the while to see where something can be added, keeping your decoration balanced.

First stick on a number of well-spaced grasses and allow them to dry before proceeding. This drying is best done by placing the pine cone in an eggcup, allowing the stalks of the grasses to rest on the rim. Once the first ring has dried you can start putting in and gluing the next.

3.6 Decorated pine cone

3.7 Pine-cone sun

Harvest dolls and animals

Dolls

Materials

- Spanish and ordinary chestnuts (conkers)
- Acorns
- Grains of corn (maize), corn leaf-sheaths and silks
- Hazelnuts
- Beechnut husks
- Rosehips
- Cocktail sticks or wooden skewers
- Copper wire
- Straw
- Sunflower seeds
- Sycamore or maple seeds

Select a few good chestnuts of the right proportions for the head and body parts of your figure.

With an awl or bodkin (or even a darning needle) make holes in the chestnuts and join them together with a piece of a cocktail stick.

Insert a piece of copper wire for the arms at the right height in the upper body (first boring a hole if necessary). The upper part of the arms can be made of acorns which should be bored beforehand; the lower part of the arms can be made of maize grains (dried corn), threaded on to the copper wire, and the hands can be made of straw. The wire enables you to bend the arms.

Make the legs from cocktail sticks inserted firmly into holes bored in the chestnut. Cut an acorn lengthwise through the middle to make a pair of shoes.

3.8 and 3.9 Harvest dolls

The woman in Figure 3.8 is finished off with an apron made from a corn leaf-sheath and some hair made from the silks.

The man has an acorn hat.

The dog is made of two acorns, a pair of sunflower seeds for ears (inserted into slits in the head) and cocktail sticks.

The materials used for the dolls in Figure 3.9 are self-evident. The basket on the woman's arm is made of half a walnut and the handle from a strip of corn leaf-sheath.

The sprig of honesty pennies in the background stands in a disc cut from a branch.

For the dolls in Figure 3.10, acorn cups, a shell from a chestnut and rosehips are used, among other things.

Acorn snake

Materials
- Acorns
- Rosehip
- Red autumn leaf
- Copper wire

Bore a little hole lengthwise in the acorn and thread the acorn on to the copper wire. Do not make the holes too big — the acorns should sit tightly on the wire.

For the eyes, carve two small eye sockets in the head and glue on two tiny pieces of rosehip peel.

Finally insert a firm red autumn leaf into the little cut-open mouth (Figure 3.11).

3.10 More Harvest dolls

3.11 Acorn snake

Pine-cone owl

1. With a piece of sandpaper flatten the bottom of the pine cone (Figure 3.12), so the owl will not fall over.

2. Take single sycamore or maple-seed wings, cut off the thick seed leaving only the wings. Stick three wings together to make each foot for the owl. When the feet are dry, glue them to the bottom of the pine cone.

With an awl, bodkin or thick needle make a hole in the beechnut and thread a piece of fine wire (florist's wire) through it to secure the beechnut (the owl's beak) between the scales of the pine cone.

3. Bind the stalks of the acorn cups together with fine wire and then using the same wire secure the two cups between the scales of the pine cone so that the beak fits nicely between the two acorn-cup eyes.

If necessary remove some of the scales to get the eyes into place.

Finally take a pine twig and secure it to the top of the pine cone with fine wire (Figure 3.13).

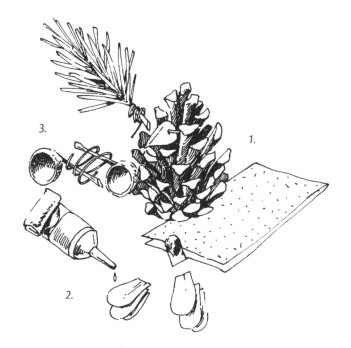

3.12 Making an owl

3.13 Pine-cone owl and mice

Pine-cone mice

The mice shown in Figure 3.13 are very simple to make. Select very pointy pine cones with the scales still closed.

Make a little hole in the bottom where the stalk joins and glue in the tail, which can be made from various materials such as wet silks twisted into a thin streamer, strands of moss or simply a thin strip of leather or a piece of wool.

The glued-on eyes can be made from a tiny twig, as with the smallest mouse; or from half a lime seed, as with the bigger mice. On the tree these seeds have a grey-green colour, but when dry they harden and turn almost black.

Winged creatures

The birds in Figure 3.14 have pine-cone or fir-cone bodies. For the heads various materials are used: an acorn with cup and stalk; a little pine cone or larch cone with a stalk. Fasten them to the body by their stalks or with a twig and glue them on, boring a hole first if necessary.

3.14 and 3.15 Winged creatures

For the wings and tail various materials are used: the wings of lime-tree seeds; the wings of maple or sycamore seeds; and little downy feathers.

The hanging bird of Figure 3.15 has real down feathers.

In Figure 3.16 chestnuts and acorns are used (follow the instructions for dolls, page 95). Flat chestnuts or half acorns are used as stands to prevent the birds from falling over. To make the wings use sycamore or maple-seed wings.

Variation

You can make a number of flying birds and assemble them to make a bird mobile, as with the plaited spirals in Figure 2.34 or attach them to a hoop as with the bee mobile in Figure 3.17.

Bee mobile

Materials
- Alder cones
- Maple or sycamore seeds
- Rattan (cane)

Cut off the seedpods from the maple-seed wings and glue the wings into the alder cones. Tie a thin thread round the middle of the bees so that they can fly.

Make a hoop from a bit of rattan. If the rattan is too pliant use two canes, gluing or tying the ends together.

Now hang the bees up at different heights on to the hoop (Figure 3.17).

3.16 More winged creatures

3.17 Bee mobile

Teasel spider

Materials

⭐ A teasel

1. A scary spider can be made from the long lower prickles of a teasel (Figure 3.18).

2. First cut off the stalk completely, then cut out the spider and hang it up on a thread.

3.18 Making a teasel spider or hedgehog

Teasel hedgehog

Materials

⭐ A teasel
⭐ Lime-tree seed cups

You can create a whole family of hedgehogs out of a few teasel heads and seeds.

Cut off some of the stalk of the teasel but leave about 5 mm (1/4 in) for its nose.

Cut away the long spidery bits round the snout and make one side flat by cutting away the prickles with a pair of scissors (Figure 3.18, step 3).

Cut a few dried black lime-tree seeds through the middle: one half is for the snout; two other halves are stuck on for the eyes.

3.19 Teasel hedgehog family

Pine-cone trolls

Materials
- ✪ Hazelnut cups
- ✪ Pine cones and fir cones
- ✪ Corn (maize) silks
- ✪ Alder cones
- ✪ Fine wire

3.20 Pine-cone trolls

The bodies of the trolls in Figure 3.20 are made from a pine cone and a fir cone.

Cut off the tops of the cones to make a flat top. Then turn the cones upside down so that the flat top becomes a base on which the cones can stand. If necessary, secure what is now the bottom row of scales with some beeswax or clay.

Select a few suitable hazelnut cups and look carefully to see which side looks most like a face.

Tie a piece of fine wire between the wild 'hairs' of the nut cups so that you can tie the head on to the body. Then tie the head on to the body with fine wire between the scales so that it cannot be seen (Figure 3.21).

For the arms you can use alder cones, inserting them with their twigs between the scales of the pine cone and gluing them in (Figure 3.21).

If there is any wire left over after attaching the head to the body use it for the arms by winding some maize silks round the wire.

For the feet, glue or tie on scales with fine wire, threading them on to the wire first before attaching them to the body. You can also fill up the hollow space at the feet with some clay to make the troll stand better. The feet of the smaller troll were made from a piece of pine cone which had been nibbled away by squirrels.

3.21 Making a troll

101

Autumn garlands

Autumn garlands can be made using all sorts of materials. While you are out walking in the country have a good look round to see what can be found in the way of ripe fruits and seeds.

Suitable materials are: fresh grains of corn (maize) and silks, dried leaves, rosehips, beechnuts and their husks, acorns and acorn cups, chestnuts, hazelnuts, straw, Spanish chestnuts, conkers and their shells, pumpkin seeds, hop cones and so on.

Mobile with autumn garlands

All the fruits, chestnuts, nuts etc. on the garlands hanging down from this mobile (Figure 3.22) are separated by little bits of straw of different lengths. To cut these, make a quick snip with a pair of very sharp scissors. If you cut too slowly, the scissors will flatten the straw and it may break.

In this example, a ring of plaited straw is used for the mobile, but other materials and forms are of course possible (Figures 2.34 and 3.17)

Window garlands

Depending on what materials you have collected, you can adorn your window. For example, thread some dried leaves carefully on to a strong thread, making sure that they are well spaced so their full shape can easily be seen. You can also use leaves which are not yet dry, but they are likely to curl up and lose their colour in a heated room. If the leaves are well dried they will generally keep their colours (see page 105 for instructions on drying leaves).

Make a loop in the thread at both ends of the garland and fix it in place with pins on to the window frame or tape it to the window itself.

If you are using corn grains, take fresh soft ones straight from the cob. If these are not available, you can boil dried grains until they become soft.

Before threading bore a little hole in the beechnut husks. Do the same for the acorns, acorn cups and hazelnuts which have already been dried. If the pumpkin seeds are still fresh and moist the needle will easily go through them, but with dried seeds you must first bore a hole.

Of course it is not necessary to hang up all the garlands at the same time as shown in Figure 3.23. Some of the fruits will slowly but surely shrivel up, so you can replace them after a while with fresh ones.

It is often nice to separate fruits and nuts with short lengths of straw so their full shape can be seen.

3.22 Mobile

Opposite: 3.23 Autumn garlands

Autumn leaf decorations

It can become an absorbing activity to look for brightly coloured autumn leaves, and many things can be made with them, especially with dried leaves. Medium-sized and smaller ones are most suitable. Collect leaves of many different shapes; when you are arranging a pattern their variety will enhance the design.

Decorating windows with fresh leaves

Materials
- ✪ Fresh autumn leaves
- ✪ Wallpaper or flour paste

Small children will nearly always want to do something right away with all the leaves they have been collecting. Something they can do is to stick the leaves on to the outside of a window with some paste. After a while the leaves will dry, shrivel up and lose their colour, but with a little warm water all the bits can be easily washed off the window.

Drying leaves

The simplest way of drying autumn leaves is to lay them in an old telephone book, and leave them for about a week. Put some heavy books or bricks on top of the telephone book to press the leaves flat. A flower or leaf press is also useful (see page 61).

Not all leaves lend themselves to being dried; some leaves, such as birch for example, lose their colour during the drying process and become quite brown. Other leaves, such as chestnut, are best picked off the tree while the inside of the leaf is still green and a little yellow-brownish edge appears round it.

Store dried leaves according to their kind, colour or size, in large envelopes. The leaves must be thoroughly dry beforehand to prevent them going mouldy.

Leaf window border

Materials
- ✪ Dried autumn leaves
- ✪ Large sheet of tracing paper
- ✪ Modelling cement or glue

Figure 3.24 shows an ornamental border made of dried autumn leaves.

Don't glue or cement the leaves directly on to the window because scraping them off again entails a lot of work (though paste can be washed off with warm water). It is also easier to make the border lying flat to try out the colour-layering and leaf combinations.

Take a large sheet of tracing paper, cut to the size of the window. Cut out the centre of the tracing paper (the border frame can also be made with strips of paper joined together). The decoration shown was made on a tracing-paper frame 10 cm (4 in) wide.

Lay out the decorations loosely on the paper so you can see when the combination is right.

Begin by arranging a number of leaves overlapping each other to make a corner. Keep rearranging the leaves until they give a pleasing appearance, but take care with them as dried leaves are brittle.

Continued overleaf

Then stick the leaves one by one to the tracing paper. Because the leaves have been dried it is best not to use a water-based paste. Modelling cement is the best: it sticks well and dries quickly. Remove surplus glue quickly.

After each item allow the glue to dry so that everything remains in place. Lay something heavy on top (such as a thick book).

If you don't want to wait while the first batch is drying, continue in another corner.

Make sure the edges of the paper are completely covered with leaves and no longer visible once the decoration is finished.

When the border is finished it can be stuck to the inside of a window with some adhesive tape.

After removing it the decoration can be stored between two sheets of card.

Harvest transparency

Materials

- ✪ Dried leaves and grasses
- ✪ Thick cardboard
- ✪ Tracing paper
- ✪ Modelling cement or glue

Cut out a frame from the cardboard. The form can be rectangular, circular or oval as desired (Figure 3.25).

Draw the outline of the frame again on the tracing paper.

Select some good leaves and/or grasses. Stick these with as little glue as possible to the tracing paper.

Finally stick the cardboard frame on to it and dry the whole thing under a weight.

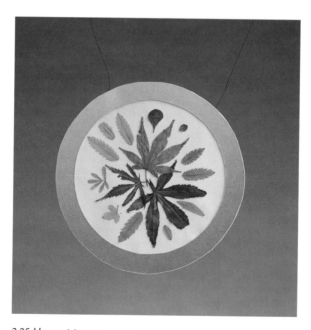

3.25 Harvest transparency

Leaf postcards and notepaper

Materials
- ✪ Dried leaves
- ✪ Card
- ✪ Sheets of notepaper
- ✪ Glue or modelling cement
- ✪ Sticky-back plastic

Figure 3.26 shows some cards and notepaper that have been simply decorated with leaves. Often you only need one beautifully shaped leaf, or you can decorate a whole side to make your own leafy postcard.

Stick the dried leaves on to the paper or card and allow them to dry under a weight.

With a picture postcard, it is better to cover the leaves with a sheet of sticky-back plastic.

3.26 Leaf postcards and notepaper

Crown of leaves

Materials
- ✪ Large dried autumn leaves, for example, sycamore or maple

Figure 3.27 shows how this crown of leaves is made.

First cut off the stems and keep them.

Lay one leaf partly over another and push a stem through them both to keep them together. Continue until the crown has reached the desired circumference.

If necessary, strengthen the crown by sticking a strip of sticky tape around the inside. Finally stick the two ends together and the crown is finished.

3.27 Crown of leaves

Michaelmas dragons

Michael and the dragon from harvest leaves

Materials
- Dried autumn leaves
- Tracing paper
- Modelling cement or glue

Making Michael and the dragon from dried leaves is similar to the window decoration in Figure 3.24. This time not only the border is decorated, but a whole picture is made (Figure 3.29).

Cut the tracing paper to fit the window frame.

First sketch out your drawing, then begin to lay out the leaves at one corner of the paper but this time without overlapping.

When each part has been glued on dry it under a weight.

Don't cover the whole sheet with leaves — leave some parts open to allow light to shine through.

Dragon loaf

Ingredients
- 500 g (18 oz) white flour, fine wheatmeal or a mixture of both
- 275 ml (10 fl oz) lukewarm milk
- $1/2$ tablespoon yeast
- 50 g ($1^3/4$ oz) hard butter
- Just under $1/2$ tablespoon salt
- Yolk of 1 egg (optional)

Measure the flour into a mixing bowl and make a hole in the middle (keep back a few spoonfuls for kneading). Dissolve the yeast into the milk, pour the mixture into the hole in the flour and stir it from the middle outwards, bringing in the flour to make a runny dough.

Cut the butter into very thin strips and lay these on top of the dough. Sprinkle the salt on to the butter.

Leave this mixture to stand for quarter of an hour until bubbles have formed. During fermentation some warmth is released and the butter is softened. Now you can lay the yolk over it. Stir it all with a fork from the middle outwards till it becomes a firm but sticky dough.

Now sprinkle the remains of the flour on to the kneading board, empty out the dough, scraping the dish. Sprinkle some flour over and knead it all to an elastic dough until it no longer sticks to the board or your hands, using more flour if necessary. Don't knead for too long, otherwise the warmth of your hands will melt the butter and the dough will become sticky.

Now put the dough back into the bowl. Put the bowl in a plastic bag or cover it with a damp cloth and allow the dough to rise to twice its volume at room temperature (1–2 hours) or in the refrigerator (3 hours or overnight). Dough which has risen cold is more easily formed.

Now shape the dough into the form of a dragon, lay it on to a baking tray and allow it once more to rise to twice its volume (loosely covered with clingfilm at room temperature). Paint the loaf with egg yolk, loosely mixed with the same amount of milk or water.

Bake for 10 minutes at 225°C, (450°F, gas mark 7–8) and then for 15 minutes at 200°C (400°F, gas mark 6).

Chestnut (conker) shell dragon

Materials
- Conker or chestnut shells
- Cocktail sticks
- Chestnut leaves
- Red berries or rosehips

Select a number of chestnut shells that are still closed. Use one that is a little open for the mouth.

Attach the shells to each other with cocktail sticks. Figure 3.28 shows what still has to be done to make the dragon look fierce. Use your imagination!

3.29 Michael and the dragon

3.28 Chestnut dragon

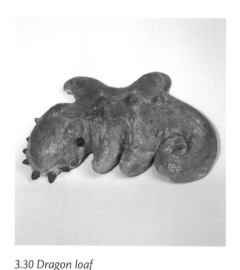

3.30 Dragon loaf

Halloween cobwebs

Materials
- A big chestnut
- Wooden skewers or cocktail sticks
- Coloured wool
- Silver thread
- An awl or large needle

3.31 *above and* 3.32–3.33 (*top and middle opposite*) *Cobwebs*

With the awl or large needle make at least seven holes round the chestnut, then insert a cocktail stick or skewer into each hole (Figure 3.31). For a large cobweb use skewers, for a small cobweb use cocktail sticks.

Select a coloured wool, tie one end on to one of the sticks and press the wool hard against the chestnut. Lead the wool from stick to stick, and round each stick. Continue until you have a thick coloured stripe.

Cut the wool, tie on another colour and continue. Make the knots as small as possible and ensure that they lie at the back of the web. The nicer side of the chestnut should be facing the front. By changing the colours you get the effect shown in Figure 3.31.

Finish off by tying the wool on to one of the sticks.

Variation 1

The cobweb in Figure 3.32 is made using the same method. This time use only one colour, and leave space between each thread, so that a real web is made.

Variation 2

The cobweb in Figure 3.33 uses silver thread, giving the appearance of dew on the cobweb.

Instead of skewers use four thin branches or canes to make a frame and drill two or three holes at intervals through each branch.

Now make a number of holes right through the chestnut.

Thrust the needle and silver thread first through a hole in one of the twigs and then through the chestnut and then again through a hole in the twig of the frame on the other side (for example from top right to bottom left). Plug the thread temporarily into the frame with broken cocktail sticks or matchsticks.

When all the threads have been attached to the chestnut, pull out a cocktail stick and pull the thread tight. Then thrust the stick firmly back into the frame and cut off the protruding bit. Repeat for each cocktail stick.

Now start weaving the web. When the cobweb is big enough tie the end with a little knot and cut off the surplus threads.

Finally you can make two holes to hang up the cobweb frame.

Halloween lantern

Materials

- Turnip or pumpkin
- Sharp knife
- Spoon
- Apple corer
- Night-light in a tin
- Wire

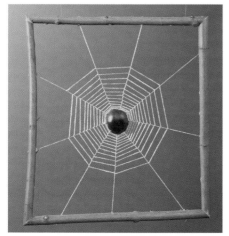

Cut a slab about 2–3 cm (1 in) thick from the top of the pumpkin or turnip.

Hollow the turnip out using a knife, spoon or apple corer. This is best done by repeatedly pushing the apple corer into the turnip and then scooping out the loose bits with a spoon. Continue until the turnip is completely hollowed out. The walls of the turnip should remain about 5–10 mm ($1/4$–$1/2$ in) thick.

Make the bottom flat, with an indentation in the middle to take the night-light.

With a sharp knife carefully carve sun, moon and stars in the outside of the turnip without cutting through the walls. Peel these designs off so that light can shine through the turnip flesh.

With the apple-corer make three holes in the lid for air, to allow the candle to burn. Insert wire through the sides of the turnip left and right and through the lid. Make the loops big enough for the lid to be opened for lighting the candle.

3.34 Halloween lantern

4. Winter

Transparencies

The basic forms are transparencies *with a cardboard frame*: these are suitable for hanging in the window, or for standing on a table. And transparencies *without a frame*: the picture is made with coloured tissue paper stuck on to tracing paper, and is suitable for hanging in a window.

When making transparencies it is best to start with a white background. A glass table with a lamp under it or a box with a light inside it are useful when making transparencies.

When choosing the colours remember that mixed colours will appear when two layers of different coloured tissue paper are laid over one another. Sometimes the result is quite surprising!

Draw the outlines on tissue paper with a sharp pencil. When you are cutting out the forms the pencil lines must be cut away too.

When cutting out the forms use a small pair of sharp scissors and take plenty of time because it is not as easy as it looks.

When gluing layers together use as little glue as possible and spread it as thinly as possible; blobs remain visible. Water-based glue is quite adequate and can be undone if necessary. However, one disadvantage is that the sheets become unstuck after a time. You can also use a glue stick.

Transparencies which are hung on the window can get damaged by condensation. Put a plastic sheet between the window and the transparency to avoid damage.

Simple transparency with a frame

These simple transparencies can be hung in front of the window. Any subject can be depicted. The simplest transparency is shown in Figure 4.1 where the picture of Easter rabbits is cut out of card and a single coloured piece of tissue paper is stuck to the back.

Draw the shape of the frame as well as the inside design on the back of a piece of strong, coloured card.

Cut out the outside frame of the transparency.

Cut out the picture inside with a pair of sharp scissors or a sharp knife.

Stick a sheet of tissue paper on to the back of the card frame (the side on which there are pencil marks).

Make a loop to hang the transparency with a needle and thread.

4.1 Simple transparency with frame

'Stained glass' transparency

This technique gives the effect of stained glass panes set in lead (Figures 4.2 and 4.3).

1. First draw the design and the frame of the transparency on white tracing paper and then transfer the forms to the (dark blue) drawing paper by using carbon paper; or you can draw the design straight on to the drawing paper (Figure 4.5).

2. Cut out the design and the framework using sharp scissors or a knife.

3. Lay tissue paper of the chosen colours on top of the drawing on the white tracing paper. The outlines of the drawing will be visible through the tissue paper. With a pencil trace the figures or details appropriate to this colour on to the tissue paper. Make the outlines on the tissue paper a little bigger than the original outlines on the drawing.

4. Cut out the figures on the coloured tissue paper and stick them on to the back of the blue drawing paper using as little glue as possible. You can use a matchstick to smear a tiny bit of glue along the edges of the drawing.

In this way stick colour by colour to the frame. When two colours of tissue paper overlap new colours are created.

Finally stick the transparency on to the window with two tiny strips of double-sided adhesive tape.

4.2 'Stained glass' transparency

4.3 'Stained glass' transparency

4.4 'Stained glass' triptych

'Stained glass' triptych

Make a simple triptych (Figure 4.4) in the same way as the previous transparency. You can put this on a table or shelf with a night-light behind it.

Once you have cut out the frame, crease it with a blunt knife or dried-up ballpoint pen to make neat folds.

Window triptych

Instead of the stained-glass window effect you can cut out a big window in the frame and fill it with several colours of tissue paper. This can be done in two ways:

1. In Figure 4.6 the boy is cut out of the card frame as a silhouette, and coloured tissue paper is added behind.

2. In Figure 4.7 Mary, Joseph and the donkey are cut out of card and then covered with tissue paper. The background is added behind.

Cut the outside shape from card and crease the folds with a blunt knife or dried-out ballpoint pen. Cut out the inside shape.

Trace the opening onto a sheet of tracing paper. Then tear the shapes you want in the background from coloured tissue paper. Stick the pieces of tissue paper on to the tracing paper and slowly build up the transparency layer by layer.

Finally cut out the tracing paper (with the design) about 1 cm ($^1/2$ in) wider than the edge of the frame, and stick it to the back of the card frame with the tissue paper to the front.

4.5 Making a stained-glass transparency

4.6 and 4.7 Window triptych

Frameless transparency

Draw the shape of the transparency on to a sheet of tracing paper. Lay it on a light table, or stick it to the window.

Figure 4.8 has been made by tearing the tissue paper. If you are not confident of making a freehand picture, draw the picture on paper and lay it under the tracing paper. Tearing the paper instead of cutting gives a very free effect. Only rarely will you need to tear a piece into an exact shape (like the sword). Using different layers and colours of tissue paper will give rich colour shadings and depth.

Layered transparencies

The technique described here uses only tissue paper, which allows the colours full scope and provides endless variations.

The angel in Figure 4.9 is made from two layers of yellow tissue paper and a layer of white tissue paper as a cover.

First draw the design onto white tracing paper.

1. Then for each layer of tissue paper draw the required part of the design onto a separate sheet of tracing paper. The yellow angel consists of the different elements shown in Figure 4.11. Lay the first sheet of yellow tissue paper on top of the first drawing and with a sharp pencil trace the figure. Cut it out.

2. Lay the cut-out sheet on the second drawing and move it around until the two drawings fit. Then lay the second sheet of yellow tissue paper exactly over the first, put the second drawing over and cut it out. Stick the two sheets together only at the edges at a few points, and do the same with the white sheet of tissue paper. Finally, stick down any loose ends with a tiny bit of glue.

4.8 Frameless transparency

4.9 Layered transparency

1.

2.

3.

4.11 Making a layered transparency

4.10 Layered transparency variation

Variation

The blue angel in Figure 4.10 has one layer more than the yellow angel (Figure 4.11, step 3): this transparency consists of two layers of light blue and one layer of pink or mauve tissue paper. The method is the same.

When sticking them together make sure that the cut-out figures fit exactly over each other; the outside edge can be trimmed later.

Candles

Dipping candles

Candles are used mainly in wintertime when it's dark, though they can be used for special occasions throughout the year. When decorating them you can choose a motif for the festival of the season.

Materials
- Beeswax or candle stubs
- Candle wick or a thick cotton yarn
- Tall narrow tins
- Pan of hot water
- Hotplate or spirit stove

Dipping candles requires a lot of patience. Hot water and molten wax are very hot! Young children should only dip candles under adult supervision.

Put some water in a saucepan to boil. Put the bits of wax or candle stubs in a tall narrow tin, and place the tin into the pan of heating water to melt the wax. The depth of the wax in the tin will determine the maximum length of the candles. When the wax has melted, the pan can be transferred to a hotplate or spirit stove on the table.

Lay some newspaper underneath to catch any spilt candle grease. Keep topping up the water to replace what has evaporated.

Wax takes a long time to melt and as it then slowly solidifies on the hotplate it is a good idea to have a second tin of melted wax ready to hand.

For the wick, cut a length of candle wick or cotton yarn long enough to prevent children getting their fingers in the hot wax. Before dipping pull the wick taut with both hands so that the finished candle will be straight.

Dip the wick into the hot wax for a moment, draw it out again and allow the wax on it to set before dipping the wick in again. In this way a new layer is added each time.

At the base of the candle a blob of wax will form and grow bigger each time the candle is dipped. Cut this blob off with a knife from time to time.

Once the candle is finished leave it to cool and harden. This can take several hours, so it is a good idea to hang the candle up by the wick to prevent it being damaged (Figure 4.12).

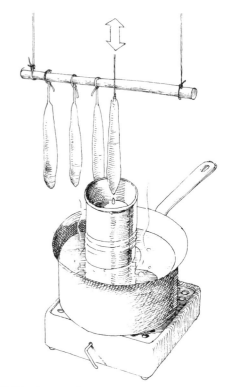

4.12 Dipping candles

Opposite: 4.13–4.18 Decorated candles

Decorating candles

Materials
- ✪ Thick candle
- ✪ Candle decorating wax in various colours
- ✪ Thick knitting needle or spatula

As you can see from Figures 4.13–4.18, candles can be decorated using various techniques. In each case the decorating wax must first be made workable.

Take small pieces and knead them well until the wax is warm and soft.

The simplest method of decorating candles is to stick little bits of coloured wax on to the candle and then work them into shape.

You can use a spatula or knitting needle to shape the finer details. New colours can be made by thoroughly kneading two different coloured bits of wax together (as for example red and yellow making orange).

Make sure that the coloured wax is properly warmed when you press it on to the candle otherwise it will not stick on properly and may come unstuck later.

Decorating candles by smearing

Materials
- ✪ Thick candle (off-white or white)
- ✪ Fine sandpaper
- ✪ Candle decorating wax in various colours
- ✪ Thick knitting needle or spatula

Use a piece of fine sandpaper to roughen the place on the candle where you wish to add the decoration.

Warm a small piece of wax between your fingers beginning with the lightest colour. Press a little wax on to the candle and smear it out very thinly with your warm fingers to give a transparent effect. Now layer the darker colours carefully over the lighter ones.

Use a knitting needle or a spatula to define the details; by scratching the wax or by pulling it up you can make forms in relief. Kneading different colours together for a long time will produce new colours.

The colours black, white, gold and silver are not transparent and so are used less in this method.

This technique requires some practice, but does give a very special effect.

Clay candlesticks

During Advent, modelling can be a wonderful occupation, and you can make candlesticks with a great variety of shapes: for instance, a simple cube, or an angel carrying a candle between the wings (Figure 4.19). Put a little saucer underneath to catch the candle wax and avoid it dripping on to the table or your clothes.

Make the candlestick out of one piece of clay. Any bits that you stick on may come unstuck when the candlestick dries.

Although you can make the candle hole to fit a particular candle, you must take the candle out of the hole while the clay is still wet because it contracts while drying and can split if the candle is left in.

Decorate the candlestick: you can stick sprigs of fir, holly, gold-painted acorns, etc. in the clay while it is still soft, and in this way it becomes a Christmas table decoration. Make sure that the sprigs are not too close to the candle flame.

Allow the candlestick to dry out thoroughly and then you can paint it with watercolours. Once the paint is dry the candlestick can be varnished.

Figure 4.20 shows a Michaelmas candlestick in the shape of a dragon.

4.20 Dragon candlestick

4.19 Cube and angel candlesticks

Advent calendars

Advent begins on the fourth Sunday before Christmas and lasts till Christmas itself. If Christmas Eve is on a Saturday, the first Sunday in Advent will fall on November 27, and Advent lasts for four full weeks. If Christmas Eve is on a Sunday, the first Sunday in Advent will fall on December 3, and the fourth Sunday of Advent coincides with Christmas Eve. Before you make an Advent calendar count the number of days in Advent in that year.

There are many kinds of Advent calendars. The most common are those in which a child opens one door for each day of Advent. Advent calendars help children anticipate Christmas, enabling them to count the days, and in some versions making the approach of Christmas visible. Advent is the festival of expectation. The colour blue can be seen to express expectation, so it is an appropriate colour for Advent.

Advent ladder

Materials

- ✪ Blue card about 25 × 35 cm (10 × 14 in)
- ✪ 2 wooden slats approximately 310 mm long x 7 mm wide (12$\frac{1}{4}$ x $\frac{1}{4}$ in)
- ✪ Gold card
- ✪ Gold paper
- ✪ Pink beeswax
- ✪ Half a walnut shell
- ✪ Unspun sheep's wool
- ✪ Glue

Round off the top corners of the blue card (Figure 4.21).

Sandpaper the slats till they are smooth and stick them to the middle of the blue card about 1 cm ($\frac{3}{8}$ in) from the bottom and 6 cm (2$\frac{3}{8}$ in) apart.

Cut two long struts 1 cm ($\frac{3}{8}$ in) wide and 31 cm (12$\frac{1}{4}$ in) long, and as many golden rungs 7 × 0.4 cm (2$\frac{3}{4}$ × $\frac{3}{16}$ in) from the gold card as there are days in Advent, including the first Sunday of Advent and Christmas Eve.

Before sticking on the rungs, mark their places on the wooden slats — the distance between each rung should be about 13 mm ($\frac{1}{2}$ in). Stick the rungs on, starting at the top and working down. Once all the rungs are firmly glued on, stick the gold card struts on to the slats so that they cover the rung-ends. Round off the tops of the struts which project beyond the slats.

Model the figure of a baby from beeswax so that it can lodge between the rungs. It is advisable to make the child from one piece rather than making limbs separately and then attaching them.

Place the walnut shell with a little sheep's wool in it at the bottom of the ladder for the crib.

From the gold paper cut out as many stars as there are days in Advent. Each day the children can stick a star on the blue sky behind the ladder as the child descends a rung. On Christmas Day the child lies in the crib, with a sky full of stars behind him.

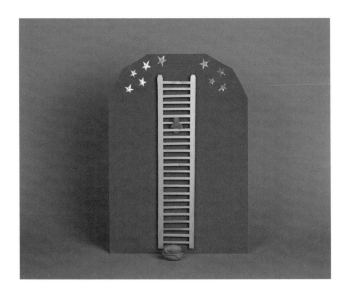

4.21 Advent ladder

Star ribbon

Materials

- ✪ 130 cm (4 ft) dark blue ribbon 2 cm (3/4 in) wide
- ✪ Silver card
- ✪ Gold card
- ✪ Straw
- ✪ Fine gold thread
- ✪ Glue

For this calendar, ribbon and stars make a kind of stairway down which an angel can come. Each Sunday in Advent is marked by a straw star and the six days between are marked by silver stars; the ladder begins with the first straw star.

As with the Advent ladder, count the number of days in Advent for the year. Stars should be made for the right number of days.

The construction of straw stars is fully described from page 141 and there is a pattern for a five-pointed star on page 130.

First lay out the straw stars and the silver card stars beside the ribbon to ensure that the distance between the stars is roughly the same.

Stick all the stars to the ribbon, making sure that you only glue the middle of the star and the points are not stuck down.

Finally, cut out an angel from the gold card. Beginning on the first Sunday of Advent, the angel comes down one step each day, and can be tucked in neatly behind the stars.

You can place a crib at the bottom of the ribbon, or you can hang the ribbon above a stable scene where at Christmas the child will be born.

Advent walnut chain

Materials

- ✪ As many walnuts as there are days in Advent
- ✪ Gold paint
- ✪ 3–4 m (yards) of red or blue ribbon 2 cm (³/4 in) wide
- ✪ Small presents to put in the nutshells
- ✪ Glue

Open the nuts carefully so you don't crack or break the shells. Remove the kernel. Keep the two halves of each nut together so that they don't get muddled up.

Paint the outside of the nutshells gold and leave them to dry. In one half of each nut place a small present such as a little bell, a dwarf, a shell, a little sheep, a little stone, a little lump of beeswax, a marble, a gold-foil star, a dried flower, a bead and so on.

Apply a little glue to each half and stick them together with the ribbon running through the two halves.

During Advent a nut is cut off the ribbon each day and opened.

Starry sky Advent calendar

Materials

- ✪ Big sheet of dark blue sugar paper or card
- ✪ Gold paper for stars
- ✪ Glue
- ✪ Scissors

Round off corners of the blue card to indicate the vault of heaven. Place the card in a suitable place: pin it to the wall, or it can form the background of a tableau for a Christmas crib.

On each day of Advent children are allowed to stick a star in the sky, forming a glorious starry sky background to the Christmas crib.

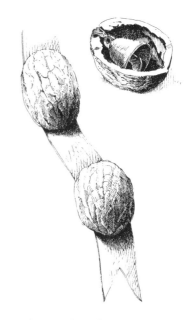

4.22 Advent walnut chain

4.23 Advent wreath

Festive wreaths

Advent wreath

Materials
- ✪ Thick wire (2 mm, 12 gauge) for the hoop
- ✪ Thin wire (1 mm, 18 gauge) for the candle holders
- ✪ Sprigs of green fir
- ✪ Waxed thread or string
- ✪ 4 candles
- ✪ Blue ribbon

1. Take a piece of thick wire, more than twice the circumference of the Advent wreath, to make a double hoop (Figure 4.24). Twist the ends firmly together.

2. Cover the frame with greenery. Start by making a foundation with larger twigs, 20–25 cm (8–10 in). Lay the bottom of the first stem against the hoop and bind it on with the waxed thread or fine string. Lay the next twig underneath the first so that it is overlapped by the first and bind it on. Continue in this way so that the wreath gradually increases in thickness.

3. After the first round use smaller sprigs which are less stiff and more easily bound on. For the last round use short pretty sprigs to give a smooth and even effect.

4. For each of the four candle holders take a piece of thin wire and wind it several times round the bottom of a candle and then bend the two ends down.

Place the candle holders on four points of the wreath, making sure that they don't disappear into the greenery but remain visible. Bend the protruding ends of wire round the bottom of the wreath (Figure 4.23).

Cut the blue ribbon in two equal lengths. Tie the ends of both ribbons on to the wreath midway between the candles. Suspend the Advent wreath by the ribbon. Alternatively you can wind the blue ribbon around the wreath as a decoration.

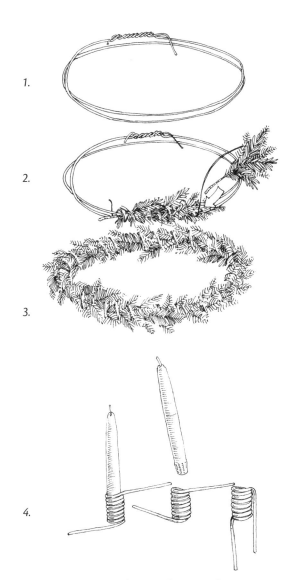

4.24 Making an advent or door wreath

Pine-cone wreath

Materials

- 7 pine cones of the same size
- Thin wire
- Ribbon
- Pliers

1. Lay the seven well-dried pine cones out in a circle and measure a length of wire 2$\frac{1}{2}$ times the circumference of the circle of cones (Figure 4.26).

2. Bend the wire double.

3. Make an eye at the bend by twisting the wire round several times. The eye is to suspend the wreath. The length of twisted wire between the eye and the first cone should be about 1 cm ($\frac{1}{2}$ in).

4. Push the wire between the scales of the first cone about a quarter of the way up from the bottom, twist the wire a few times so that the pine cone sits firmly between the wires.

5. Attach the other cones in the same way.

Make sure you twist the wire sufficiently between each cone so that they are not too close together, otherwise you will not be able to bend the wire round to make a wreath.

Once all seven cones have been attached, bend the whole thing round to make a wreath. Twist the end of the wire a few times round the eye and cut off.

Finish off the wreath by tying a bow with ribbon under the eye (Figure 4.25). You could also tie in some greenery.

4.25 Pine-cone wreath

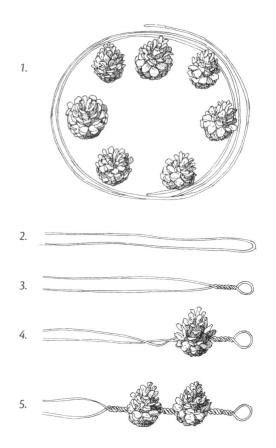

4.26 Making a pine-cone wreath

Door wreath

4.27 Door wreath

Materials
- Waxed thread or string
- Fir sprigs
- Coniferous greenery
- Wire 1.5 mm (15 gauge)
- Decoration, such as holly leaves, ivy, berries, pine and larch cones, lichen

Make a ring of wire about 25 cm (10 in) in diameter, twisting the ends firmly together (Figure 4.27). First attach some larger fir sprigs (20–25 cm, 8–10 in long) as described for the Advent wreath (Figure 4.24).

Use plenty of greenery and pull the wire tight. Avoid protruding twigs. After the foundation of fir twigs continue with coniferous greenery until the wreath has been built up evenly all round. Continue building the wreath using the wire for support and covering any visible parts of the wire. Use smaller sprigs of greenery and arrange them evenly with an overlap. Pay attention to the blend of colours.

Attach pine cones, larch cones, berries and lichen, by winding a 15 cm (6 in) piece of wire under the lowest row of scales on the cone. Pull the wire tight and twist it round a few times with a pair of pliers before binding it to the wreath. Lichen can be attached similarly.

Finally tie a coloured ribbon to the wreath by which it can be suspended.

Lanterns

A simple lantern

Materials
- ✪ Thin drawing paper (120 gsm)
- ✪ Watercolours and brush
- ✪ Salad oil
- ✪ Glue
- ✪ Wide jam jar
- ✪ Candle

The lantern consists of a loose cuff of paper placed over the jam jar (Figure 4.28, step 1).

Wet the paper, lay it on a board and smooth it out by wiping a wet sponge over it.

Paint the wet paper with watercolours. Don't paint a picture, just create a mood with the colours.

Allow the paper to dry and oil both sides of the paper sparingly with cooking oil.

Cut the paper to the right size. The depth of the paper should be slightly more (but not more than 1 cm, 1/2 in) than the height of the glass. The length of the paper should be about 2 cm (3/4 in) more than the circumference of the glass.

Glue the ends of the paper together to make a cylinder which will fit easily over the glass jar.

Place a night-light or a small candle in the jar and the lantern is finished.

Variation

Instead of the jar use a round Camembert cheese box. Cut away half of the (usually high) rim and remove the top of the lid (Figure 4.28, step 2).

Glue the upper and lower rims and stick the painted paper first to the bottom half and then to the top half of the cheese box. Finally glue the vertical edges of the paper together.

Take a strip of aluminium foil, fold it several times, and wrap it round a small candle, so that it extends below the candle. Make several cuts in the foil so that it can be spread open in rays and glue them to the bottom of the lantern.

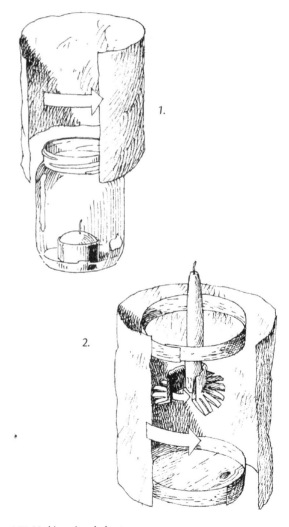

4.28 Making simple lanterns

Glass jar lantern

Materials
- ✪ Large glass jar (2 litre, 2 quarts)
- ✪ Tissue paper in various colours
- ✪ Gold card
- ✪ An old cloth
- ✪ Wallpaper paste
- ✪ Sharp knife or needle

Glue a layer of white tissue paper around the outside of the jar as a base for the transparency. It does not need to be smooth all over.

Copy the picture in Figure 4.29 or sketch your own design on a piece of paper. Don't make the figures too small.

Tear or cut the garments out of tissue paper. Stick the figures flat on the white tissue paper. Put a fold or two in the clothes. Kings can have golden crowns on their heads and even golden staffs in their hands.

Use blue tissue paper for the sky. To make a starry sky scratch out stars here and there with a sharp knife or big needle.

A large jar needs a bigger candle. A night-light is too dim.

4.29 Glass jar lantern

Star lantern

Materials
- ✪ Strong drawing paper (170 gsm)
- ✪ Pair of compasses or protractor
- ✪ Ruler
- ✪ Craft knife
- ✪ Night-light
- ✪ Glue stick

This lantern is made up of 11 pentagons. Use the pattern in Figure 4.31 to cut out the size you require.

You can paint the paper with watercolours before drawing the pentagons and cutting them out.

Continued overleaf

4.30 Star lantern

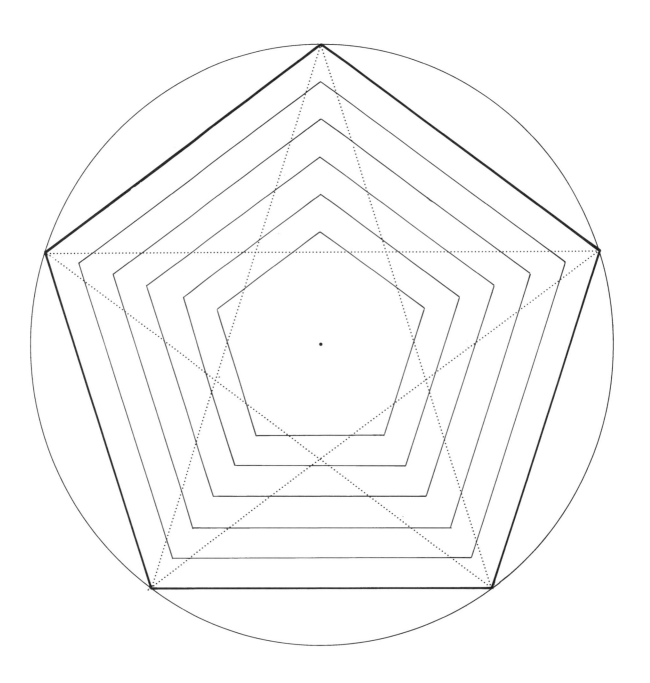

1. Bisect all the sides of the pentagons. Join these points together, scoring along the lines lightly with a knife (Figure 4.32).

2. Fold in the triangles you have made to make a smaller pentagon.

3. Stick the pentagons together in such a way that the flaps — the folded corners — always overlap the adjoining pentagon.

4. First construct the bottom half from the base and then build up the upper edge by sticking the pentagons point downward on to the bottom half. For the opening at the top, stick the flaps down inside. Do the same at the bottom if you don't wish to have a base; without a base the candle or night-light is more easily lit.

When the candle is lit inside the lantern, a five-pointed star becomes visible in every pentagon (Figure 4.30).

Opposite: 4.31 Pentagons

Right: 4.32 Making a star lantern

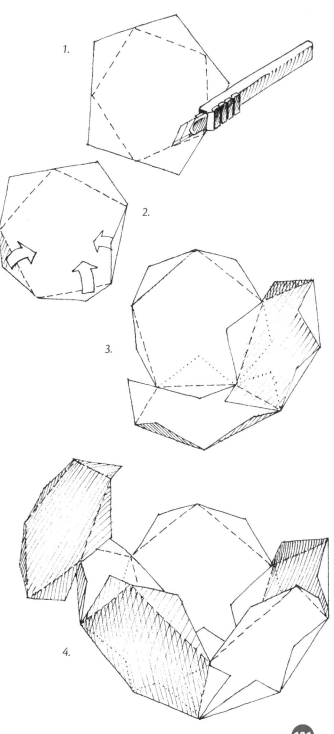

Dodecahedron lantern

Materials
- ✪ Strong drawing paper (160 gsm)
- ✪ Pair of compasses or protractor
- ✪ Ruler
- ✪ Craft knife
- ✪ Glue stick

This lantern looks like the star lantern, but without the 5-pointed stars.

Make smaller pentagons with sides of 5 cm (2 in). The pattern in Figure 4.30 gives you an exact pentagon. Figure 4.105 (page 164) shows (at 60% of true size) how to cut several pentagons from one sheet, to save sticking them together (ignore the odd sixth one in Figure 4.105).

1. Cut out two lots of five pentagons, adding extra flaps at *a* (Figure 4.33). Fold the flaps inwards and glue them to each other. In this way they are invisible when the light shines through.

2. Stick the pentagons of the top and bottom halves together by folding their flaps inward in the same way.

This lantern can be painted before drawing and cutting out the pentagons or it can be covered with tissue paper (Figure 4.34).

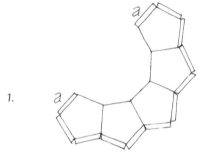

1.

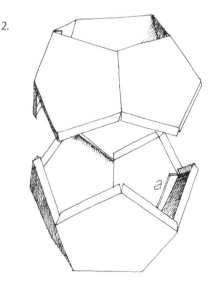

2.

Right 4.33 Making a dodecahedron

Above 4.34 Dodecahedron lantern

Angels

Woollen angel

4.35 Woollen angel

1. When working with upspun sheep's wool, don't cut it but gently tease it apart (Figure 4.36).

2. Separate off one third of the wool for the arms and wings of the angel.

3. Tie a knot in the middle of the thicker skein and pull it tight. This becomes the face.

4. Hold the skein vertically, letting the wool above the knot fall down.

5. Spread this wool round the head as hair and secure at the neck with a long gold thread. Tie the ends of the gold thread together to make a loop for suspending the figure.

6. Lay the angel face down. Take the wool which you have just brought down for hair and divide it into three parts. Bring the middle part back up over the head; bring the other two parts to the sides — they will shortly become the wings.

7. For one of the arms separate off a bit of wool about 15 cm (6 in) long from the thin skein. Twist the wool firmly together in the middle, fold the skein double and tie up the hand with gold thread. Do not cut off the fluff forming the arms. Make the other arm in the same way.

8. Keeping the angel face down, place the arms under the neck and bring the tuft of wool which you laid over the head down over the arms.

9. Turn the angel over, push the arms and wings well up, and tie up the body firmly under the arms with a length of gold thread. Allow the ends to hang down as tassels from the belt.

Fluff the wings and robe into shape by holding the wool firmly in one hand and teasing it out carefully with the other (Figure 4.35).

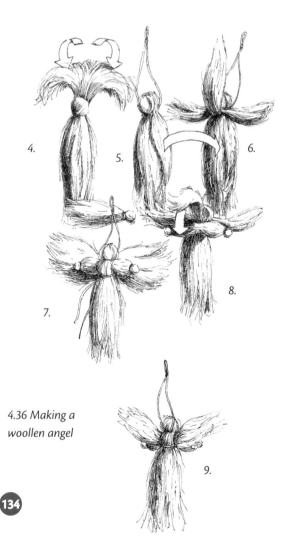

Angel mobile

Materials

- ✪ White tissue paper
- ✪ Unspun sheep's wool
- ✪ Gold thread
- ✪ White yarn
- ✪ Fine silver wire
- ✪ Walnut shell
- ✪ White beeswax
- ✪ Glue
- ✪ Scissors
- ✪ Pliers

Cut out two squares 18 × 18 cm (7 × 7 in) from tissue paper. Lay one of the squares shiny side down on the table with one of the corners pointing away from you (Figure 4.37).

1. Fold the left and right corners 2.5 cm (1 in) inwards.

2. Put a blob of wool the size of a big marble in the middle of the square.

3. Fold the paper over the blob so that the two opposite corners meet.

4. Shape the blob and tie off the head with white thread.

5. Make hands out of the two corners of the paper and tie them up with white thread. Give the angel shape, making the upper part billow out so that she really appears to sweep through the air.

Take two lengths of gold thread 20 cm (8 in) and tie each end to a hand (Figure 4.38). Tie the other ends of the threads together and glue them to the rim of the walnut shell. Take care that the threads are of equal length.

Make a second angel in the same way and glue the threads to the other side of the walnut.

1.

2.

3.

4.

5.

6.

7.

8.

4.36 *Making a woollen angel*

9.

Cut a length of 17 cm (7 in) from the silver wire and bend back both ends of the wire with pliers to make loops. Bend the wire to make a slight bow. Tie a gold thread about 17 cm (7 in) long round the neck of both angels, and tie these threads to the wire loops. Tie a gold thread to the middle of the wire to suspend the mobile.

Stuff a tuft of wool into the walnut shell (which can be painted gold) and lay a little beeswax child in it. Now the angels can bear the child down from heaven to the earth.

You could make the angels independently, or alternatively make a mobile with more angels.

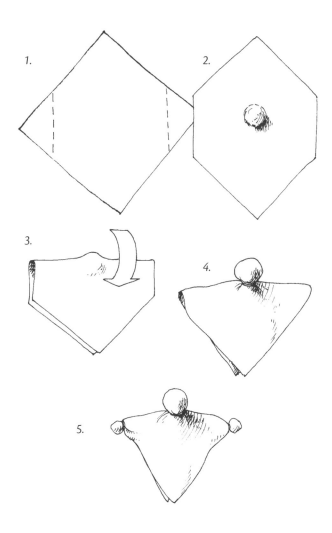

4.37 Making a paper angel

4.38 Angel mobile

Straw angel

See page 141 for various ways of preparing straw.

For the *head* and *body* use un-ironed round straw.

For the *arms* use ironed straw.

For the *wings* use straw which has been cut open and ironed flat.

Take about eight un-ironed round stalks and allow them to soak in a basin of water for several hours to make them more pliant. Follow the steps in Figure 4.40.

1. Bend the straw over in the middle. The length of the halved straws now makes up the head, body and lower half of the angel.

2. Tie off the head with a strong thread.

3. Take three or four ironed (not cut open) straws and insert them between the round straws of the body to form the arms.

4. Tie off the body.

5. Now form the straws which make up the lower part of the angel into a round bell shape using something round, for example a medicine bottle or a candle (diameter 1.5–2 cm, 3/4 in). Insert it into the bottom of the bell of straws, so that the wet straws are made to stand out. Stick the straw on to the medicine bottle with adhesive tape that can be removed easily afterwards.

Allow the straw to dry overnight in this position and next day remove the tape. The straw will now form a round bell shape.

6. Trim the bottom with scissors, but don't cut too much off. Test whether the angel will stand properly by placing her on the table.

Finish off the arms by gluing the arm straws together and bending them forward before the glue dries.

At this point the angel should still have very long arms. In fact you can now tie these arms together with a bit of string to hold them in front. Once the glue is completely dry trim the arms to the proper length and make hands by tying the ends of the straw together with thread.

7. While the angel's body is drying you can make the wings. Take flat, opened stalks of the same colour. Lay them across each other in a fan shape and glue them together. Dry them under pressure, so that the fan is as flat as possible. You can use adhesive tape here to keep the wings in shape.

Before attaching the wings, dress the angel with a girdle made of a strip of gold foil (Figure 4.39), with two golden bands crossing over the breast, or with a golden headband which can have a star.

8. Glue the fan on to the back of the angel's body to form the wings. When the glue is dry clip the wings to the correct shape.

The number of straw stems determines the thickness of the angel. Don't use less than eight stalks for the body or the lower part will be too thin.

Opposite, near right: 4.39 Straw angel

Opposite, far right: 4.40 Making a straw angel

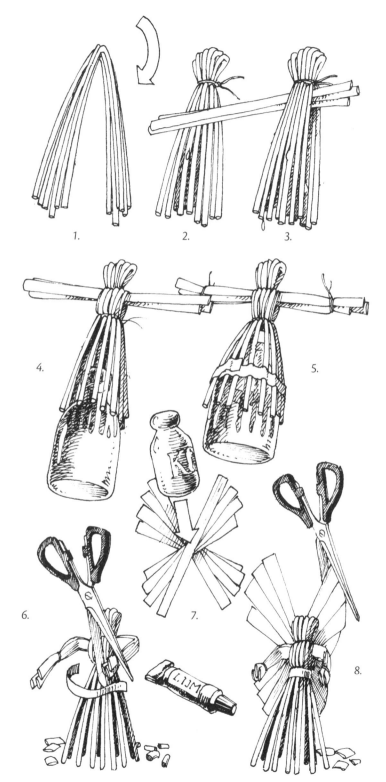

1.

2.

3.

4.

5.

6.

7.

8.

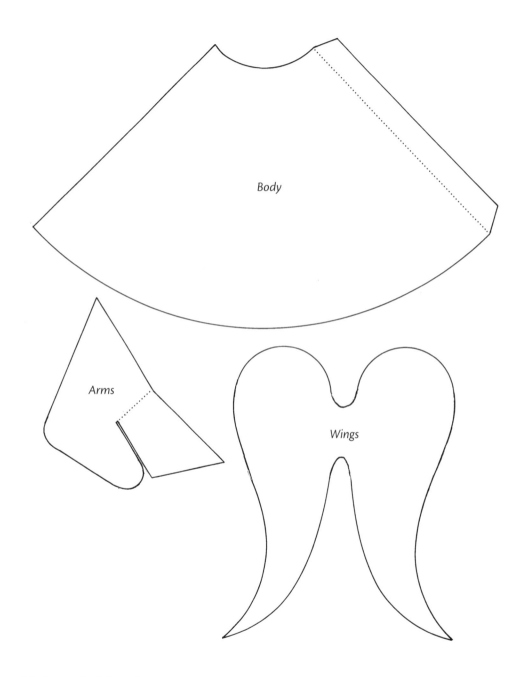

Body

Arms

Wings

4.41 Pattern for foil angel

Foil angel

4.42 Foil angel

Start by cutting out the pieces for the body, arms and wings from gold foil (Figure 4.41). Now follow the steps in Figure 4.43.

1. Cut a square piece of tissue paper 10 × 10 cm (4 × 4 in) for the head. Place a small ball of unspun sheep's wool in the centre.

2. Fold the paper over the ball to make a head.

3. Tie the head at the neck with thread.

4. To decorate the foil body and wings as shown in Figure 4.42, lay the foil with the shiny outside facing up on a base of soft cardboard. Draw shapes on using a blunt needle or a fine knitting needle.

5. Attach the head by placing the neck inside the body and sticking the two edges of the body together to make a funnel shape.

6. Stick the arms to both sides of the body, and the wings to the back. Take a little tuft of teased sheep's wool, spread this round the head for hair and glue it on. Finally make two little hands of tissue paper and stick these to the arms.

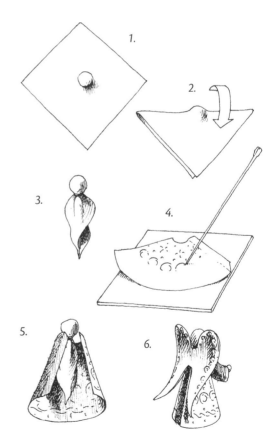

4.43 Making a foil angel

Straw stars

Materials
- ✪ Natural-coloured straw
- ✪ Sharp knife
- ✪ Pointed scissors
- ✪ Basin of water
- ✪ An iron

Soak the straw in water for about an hour. For flat straw, cut down into the tops a little way with a sharp knife and iron them open further with a hot iron. You can also leave the wet straws uncut and hollow, and just iron them flat.

You can use both flat and hollow stalks, and make them into very wide or very narrow strips (cut with a ruler and a sharp knife). Straw stars made of flat straws have the disadvantage that they have a good side and a bad side, so they look best against a background.

Straw stars made from hollow straw are the same on both sides, and are more suitable for mobiles, for use on the Christmas tree or to be hung in front of a window.

In the examples given in this book gold thread is always used for suspending the stars, but any other colour can be used, for instance, red.

Cut the stalks into two or three lengths depending on the size of the star.

8-pointed star

1. Lay two stalks of equal length crosswise upon each other (Figure 4.53).

2. Add another two diagonal stalks. Put your forefinger on the point where the stalks cross each other to hold them in place and weave a thread round the stalks, taking it first over the topmost straw, then under the next, then over the one after that, and so on.

3. Finally tie the two ends of the thread together behind the star.

Alternatively, you could lay the straw crosswise on a block of wood and pin it down so you have both hands free to bind the straws together.

Cut the points of the stars to your preferred shape (Figure 4.54).

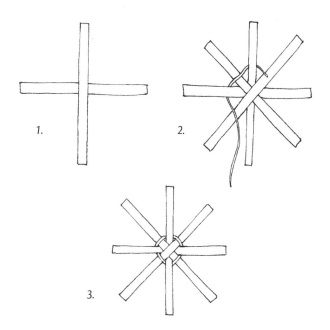

Opposite: 4.44–4.52 Various straw stars

4.53 Making an 8-pointed star

16-pointed star

Make two 8-pointed stars (Figure 4.44 and 4.53) and lay one on top of the other. Bind the stars together with a thread in the same way as described on page 141. The thread of one of the eight-pointed stars can be cut away.

With practice you can make this star by laying all eight stalks on top of each other at the same time, working the thread through them all and tying it up.

Altering the length and width of the stems will vary the result. Stars with a greater number of points can be made. By alternating wide and narrow, short and long, flat and hollow straw you can make innumerable varieties (Figures 4.44–4.52).

16-pointed star with 8 little stars

This star consists of four short and four long flat stems of straw (Figure 4.55). Select four wide stems and take three narrower ones for each of the eight surrounding stars (the fourth straw being already formed by the long straws of the central star).

Make an 8-pointed star with narrower straws, and tie it over the centre star.

With skill this combined star can be extended even further.

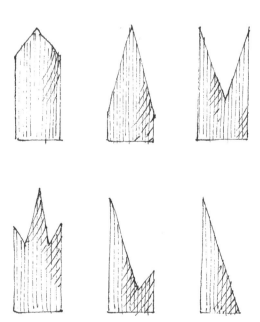

4.54 Star points

4.55 16-pointed star with 8 little stars

12-pointed star

1. Cut two flat stems into three pieces each. First lay three pieces on top of each other (Figure 4.56).

2. Then add the other three pieces as shown in the diagram.

3. Make sure the first straw (at the bottom) is vertical, and the last straw is horizontal so that the first and last straw make a cross enclosing the other straws.

The thread with which the star is woven together comes from behind and goes over the last laid straw, under the next straw and so on.

Stars with 24 and 32 points

For the star with 24 points lay one 12-pointed star on another (Figure 4.56), weave a thread through them and tie them together. Cut off the surplus thread.

Figure 4.50 shows a large and a small star combined to make a star with 24 points.

Variation with 24 points

The star in Figure 4.52 uses three wide and nine long narrow straws. Follow the steps in Figure 4.57.

1. Lay the three wide straws on top of each other.

2. Lay the three narrow straws behind them.

3. Lay two straws on top in the gaps between the narrow and the wide straws.

Finally bind them together.

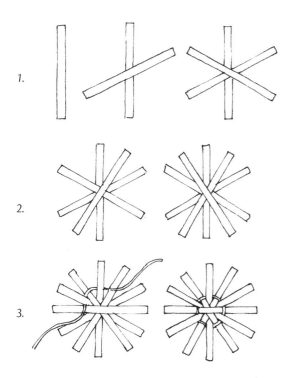

4.56 Making a 12-pointed star

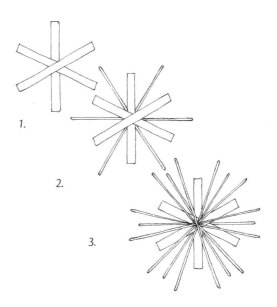

4.57 Variation on a 24-pointed star

Variation with 32 points

This star is made in the same way as the one above, except that two stars with sixteen points are used. A similar star can be made from four 8-pointed stars. (Figures 4.51, 4.58–4.60)

Great star with 64 points

Figure 4.61 is made with 32 whole (unironed) stems of straw. In this case the straw is worked while still wet, as it is more pliable and breaks less easily.

Make a star from eight stalks by laying them crosswise on top of each other and tying them up. Make a second star in the same way.

Lay one star on top of the other, so that the rays interlock. Tie the star together with a new thread. The result is a star with 32 points.

Make a second star with 32 points, lay one star on top of the other and tie them together with new thread, to make a star with 64 points.

The straw must still be wet when you finish the ends.

4.58–4.60 32-pointed stars

4.61 Great star

Straw-star mobile

The mobile in Figure 4.62 has a large star of David with twelve 12-pointed stars. This mobile can be hung during the time between Christmas and Epiphany (January 6). Begin with the large star of David and each day add a 12-pointed star.

For the star of David take six wet whole straws.

1. Lay three straws on top of each other to make an equilateral triangle and tie the ends together (Figure 4.63). With the other three straws make another triangle.

2. Lay one triangle on top of the other to make the 6-pointed star of David. Tie the stars together where they cross and suspend the mobile from four points (Figure 4.62).

Make the 12-pointed stars from whole straws ironed flat: since these are heavier they hang well.

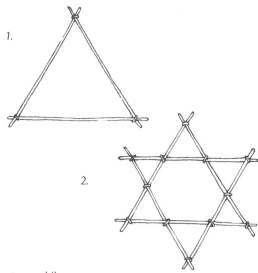

4.62 Straw-star mobile

4.63 Making a star of David

Paper window stars

Transparent window stars are made by folding each piece of paper into a single star-point and then assembling these star-points into a star.

Kite paper (transparency paper) is sufficiently transparent and is more robust than tissue paper, so it is more easily worked.

Tissue paper is less colour fast than kite paper and since transparent stars are usually left to hang for a long time, tissue-paper stars can quickly lose their colour in the increasing strength of the sunlight.

When choosing the colours remember that the patterns emerge from layering different colours of paper. For complicated stars dark colours are not suitable; use yellow, orange, pale green or pink.

Do not make the stars too small because it is more difficult to make the folds exact. The examples in this book have a diameter of 20 cm (8 in).

The proportion of the sheets is important — if altered, the pattern changes too. For example Figure 4.76 uses 10 × 7.5 cm (4 × 3 in) sheets while Figure 4.77 uses 10 × 4.5 cm (4 × 1³/4 in) sheets.

Before making the star-points experiment with:
Rectangular sheets (for instance 10 × 7.5 cm, 4 × 3 in). Here the length of the sheet determines the dimensions of the star. In our examples (page 151) the star will be twice the length, that is 20 cm (8 in).
Square sheets where the diagonal determines the

dimensions of the star. A sheet 7.5 × 7.5 cm (3 × 3 in) has a diagonal of a little over 10 cm (4 in) — about one third longer than the sides.

4.64 Square sheet

Work out beforehand how many pieces can be obtained from one large sheet to avoid waste. You can get 100 rectangular sheets (10 × 7.5 cm, 4 × 3 in) or 130 square sheets (7.5 × 7.5 cm, 3 × 3 in) out of a 75 × 102 cm (30 × 40 in) sheet of kite paper.

Make sure that the pieces are exactly the same size; to achieve this, first fold the large sheet exactly in half (with a sharp crease) and slit in two with a sharp knife. Then fold these sheets in two and cut them. Continue in this way until you have obtained the desired size. A guillotine or trimmer is very useful for this. In order to obtain a different shape of sheet, narrower, wider or longer, first cut a strip off the large sheet, so that exact measurements are obtained.

It is important to fold the sheets as exactly as possible because any divergence shows up in the final result.

The creases must be really sharp. When the same points have to be folded twice as in Figure 4.78 then don't make the first fold come exactly to the centre line but leave a tiny gap. Ensure that the sides come exactly together with the second fold.

Stick down all the folded parts using transparent glue or a glue stick. Non-transparent glue becomes visible when the star is hung up. Make sure that you don't use too much glue on the paper.

Finally stick the stars to the window with strips of double-sided adhesive tape. Use only very small strips and stick them to the parts where the star is least transparent (the points) then the tape will not be seen. Large pieces of tape will make the star difficult to remove without damage.

Stars from square pieces

With stars made from square pieces the diagonal is the central fold.

Simple 8-pointed star

8 pieces of kite paper (7.5 × 7.5 cm, 3 × 3 in)

1. Fold the sheets across the diagonal so that points B and C meet. Unfold again (Figure 4.65).

2. Fold points B and C in to the diagonal; stick them down with a spot of glue.

3. When all eight sheets are folded in this way stick the star carefully together, with the unfolded base of the first star-point to the diagonal of the next, continuing until all the points have been stuck together (Figure 4.69).

10-pointed star

10 pieces of kite paper (7.5 × 7.5 cm, 3 × 3 in)

Fold the star-points in the same way as before (Figure 4.65, steps 1 and 2).

Stick the unfolded base of the second star-point a little bit over the diagonal of the first as in Figure 4.66, step 2. This forms a pattern of rays in the heart of the star (Figure 4.70).

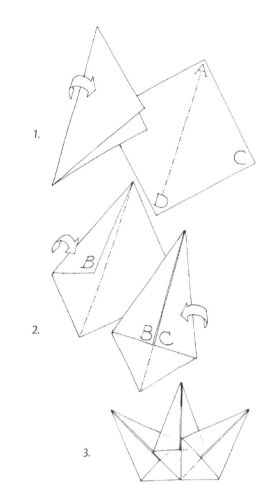

4.65 Making a simple star

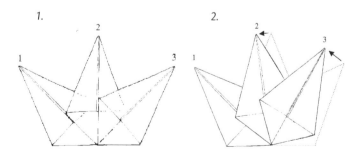

4.66 Making a 10-pointed star

8-pointed star

8 pieces of kite paper (7.5 × 7.5 cm, 3 × 3 in)

This 8-pointed star is a slight variation (Figure 4.67).

1. Crease the diagonal, fold points *B* and *C* to the diagonal.

2. Unfold again.

3. Fold points *B* and *C* to the newly made crease, close the flaps again, and stick down securely.

Then stick the star together as in Figure 4.65, step 3 to result in Figure 4.71.

5-pointed star

5 pieces of kite paper (7.5 × 7.5 cm, 3 × 3 in)

By taking five instead of eight star-points you can modify the star in Figure 4.71 to make Figures 4.72 and 4.73.

The overlap of each individual point of the star is no longer a half point as before, but only about 10–12 mm, 1/2 in (Figure 4.68). In this way a five-point motif appears in the middle (Figure 4.72).

10-pointed star

10 pieces of kite paper (7.5 × 7.5 cm, 3 × 3 in)

With ten star-points make two 5-pointed stars and stick one on top of the other. This gives you the star in Figure 4.73.

Alternatively first assemble one 5-pointed star and then stick the remaining five points one by one between the points of the star.

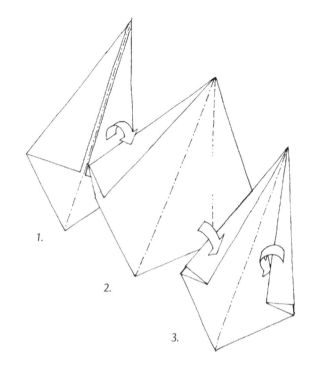

4.67 Making an 8-pointed star

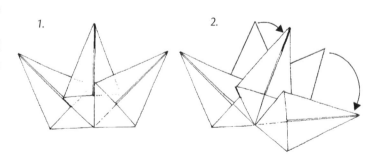

4.68 Making a 5-pointed star

4.69 Simple 8-pointed star

4.70 10-pointed star

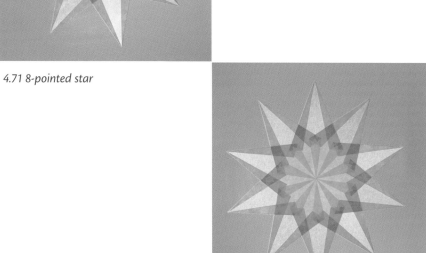

4.71 8-pointed star

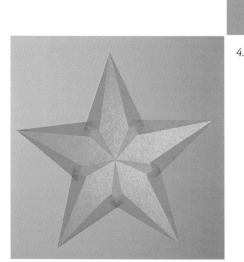

4.72 5-pointed star

4.73 10-pointed star

4.74 11-pointed star

11-pointed star

11 pieces of kite paper (7.5 × 7.5 cm, 3 × 3 in)

Fold the sheets as in Figure 4.67, steps 1 and 2.

1. Then fold the lower half (the part that will become the centre of the star) towards the diagonal line (Figure 4.75).

2. Stick the folds down.

Stick the 11 star-points together to produce the star of Figure 4.74.

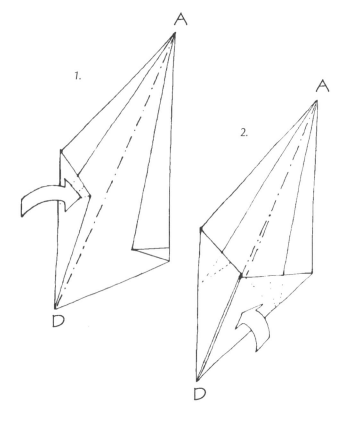

4.75 Making an 11-pointed star

Stars from rectangular pieces

With rectangular sheets, the length of the sheet determines the dimensions of the star. Thus the diameter of the star will be 20 cm (8 in) using sheets of 10 × 7.5 cm (4 × 3 in).

Two simple 8-pointed stars

Star 1

8 pieces of kite paper (10 × 7.5 cm, 4 × 3 in)

1. Fold the sheets lengthwise and unfold them again (Figure 4.78).
    2. Fold the four corners in to the centre line so that a point is made above and below. Stick down the corners with glue.
    3. From the top point fold the two sides once again to the centre line. This sharp point makes one of the points of the star, while the wider lower point will be in the centre of the star.
    4. When all eight sheets have been folded in this way stick the star carefully together, with the unfolded base of the first star-point to the diagonal of the next, continuing until all the points have been stuck together (Figure 4.76).

Star 2

8 pieces of kite paper (10 × 4.5 cm, 4 × 1³/4 in)

Fold in the same way as above, but with the narrower sheet, you will get the star in Figure 4.77.

Continued overleaf

4.76 Simple 8-pointed star (Star 1)

4.77 Simple 8-pointed star (Star 2)

8-pointed star variations

Star 1

8 pieces of kite paper (10 × 7.5 cm, 4 × 3 in)

1. Fold the sheets lengthwise and unfold them again (Figure 4.80).

2. Fold the two top corners in to the centre line. Unfold them again.

3. Halve the corner folds and tuck the edge inside as you fold it again.

4. Assemble the star by first using four star-points to make a 4-pointed star. Then insert the remaining points between the gaps.

Above: 4.79 8-pointed star (star 1)
Below: 4.83 8-pointed star (star 2)

4.78 Making a rectangular 8-pointed star

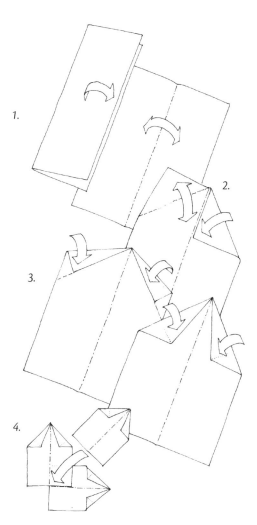

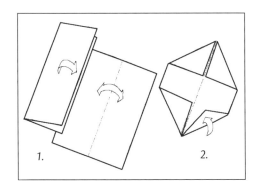

4.80 Making star 1

4.81

Star 2

8 pieces of kite paper (10 × 7.5 cm, 4 × 3 in)

Fold each corner towards the centre line (Figure 4.81). Now follow Figure 4.82.

1. Unfold the lower corners again.

2. Fold the lower two points to the new crease and then fold inwards.

3. Fold the top flap onto the centre crease.

4. Finish by folding the other flap.

Stick together to make the star in Figure 4.83.

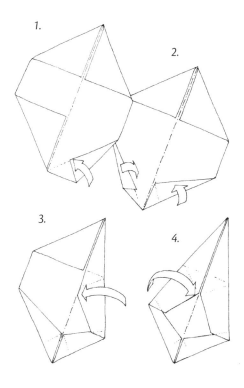

4.82 Making star 2

4.84 8-pointed star (star 3)

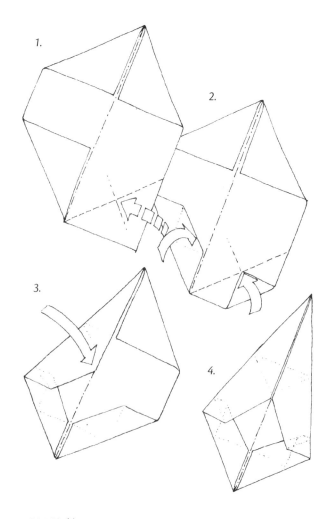

4.85 Making star 3

Star 3

8 pieces of kite paper (10 × 7.5 cm, 4 × 3 in)

Fold each corner towards the centre line (Figure 4.81). Now follow Figure 4.85.

1. Unfold the lower corners again. Find the midpoint of the fold line by folding carefully diagonally.

2. Then fold the outer point to the midpoint of the fold line and refold both sides along the fold line to the middle.

3. Fold the top flap onto the centre crease.

4. Finish by folding the other flap.

Stick together to make the star in Figure 4.84.

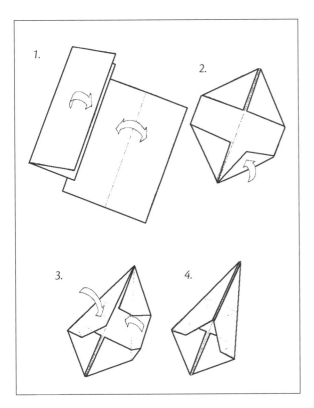

4.86 Folding a 16-pointed star

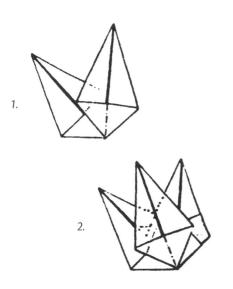

4.87 Assembling a 16-pointed star

16-pointed star

16 pieces of kite paper (10 × 7.5 cm, 4 × 3 in)

Choose a light colour as there are many layers of paper on top of each other in this star.

Fold the pieces as in Figure 4.86, then follow Figure 4.87.

1. Stick the star-points as if making an 8-pointed star.

2. Then stick one star-point exactly between each of the eight. The result can be seen in Figure 4.88.

4.88 16-pointed star

Narrow 8-pointed star

8 pieces of kite paper (12 × 4.5 cm, 4³/4 × 1³/4 in)

This star looks quite different because the sheets are narrower. Don't use sheets smaller than the above measurements as they will be too difficult to work.

Follow the basic folds in Figure 4.86. Then follow the steps in Figure 4.89.

1. Fold the outside folds again.
2. Then fold them again to make a sharp point.

Stick together to make the star in Figure 4.90.

4.90 Narrow 8-pointed star

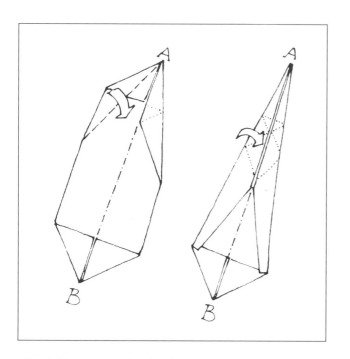

4.89 Making a narrow 8-pointed star

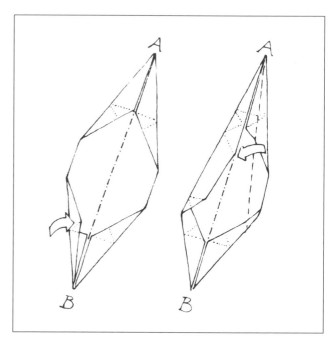

4.92 Making Star 2

156

4.91 Narrow 16-pointed star (Star 1)

Narrow 16-pointed stars

Star 1

6 pieces of kite paper (15 × 4.5 cm, 6 × 1³/4 in)

Fold the star-points in the same way as for the Narrow 8-pointed star.

Stick the star together as described for the previous 16-pointed star (Figures 4.87 and 4.88).

The final result can be seen in Figure 4.91.

Star 2

16 pieces of kite paper (15 × 4.5 cm, 6 × 1 ³/4 in)

In this star an extra fold is added and so a larger size of paper is used (Figure 4.92).

1. Fold each of the corners twice.

2. Then fold the two outside corners in again to make a sharp point.

Stick together like the previous version (Figures 4.87 and 4.88) to make the star in Figure 4.93.

4.93 Narrow 16-pointed star (Star 2)

Nativity scenes

Clay stable

A clay stable can be made as simply as you wish (Figure 4.94). Children can make this stable by themselves.

With these simple stables the surrounding landscape creates an atmosphere. Use dark brown or green cloth and lay some stones, moss or pine cones on it. Make trees by sticking a sprig of green in a lump of clay.

You could let the children make something for each Sunday during Advent:

On the first Sunday make the stable.

On the second Sunday make some bushes and trees to go round it.

On the third Sunday make some sheep.

And on the fourth Sunday the people: Joseph, Mary and the shepherds, and for Christmas, the angel and the child.

Make the figures in one piece. Do not make arms, legs and head and then stick them on to the body because once the clay dries the separate parts are likely to fall off.

Once the stable is dry it can be painted if desired.

4.94 Clay stable

Nativity scene

Materials
- ✪ White and brown unspun sheep's wool
- ✪ Pink cotton knit
- ✪ Coloured scraps of cloth and felt
- ✪ Scraps of fur
- ✪ Unspun wool or camel hair

Nativity figures

1. For each figure work a tuft of teased white wool into a firm roll approximately 9 cm (3¹/2 in) long (Figure 4.95).

2. Form a round head at one end.

3. Wrap a piece of cotton knit round it and tie it off to make the head.

4. Make a fairly close-fitting garment from a thicker woollen material or felt to cover the rest of the roll of wool, so that the figure can stand.

5. Gather the cloth in at the neck.

Mary has a robe of red felt, with a cloak made of a square piece of blue cloth or felt.

6. Drape the cloak round her head and fasten with a few stitches at the head and the neck.

7. The hands are made of some teased sheep's wool covered with cotton knit. Sew them to the inside of the cloak.

Draw in the eyes and mouth with a fine pencil.

Joseph and the shepherds have capes of cloth or fur. Secure these at the neck and at the centre front with a few stitches. A stick can then be inserted between the cape and the body (Figure 4.95, step 7).

The hair is made of teased brown sheep's wool secured with the hat.

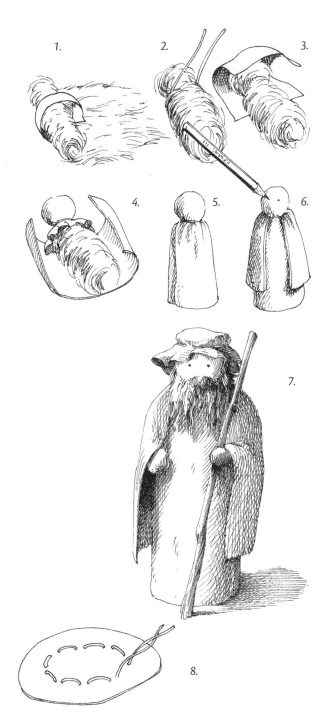

4.95 *Making nativity figures*

8. The hat is made from a round piece of felt. You can shape the hat by gathering it, then sew it on to the head with a few stitches.

The *child* is made in the same way as the other dolls, only a little smaller. When the head is finished wrap the rest of the body in a cloth of light-coloured material, flannel or felt. Secure the cloth with a few stitches.

Make a simple *sheep* from a rectangular piece of fur or fleece. Roll this in from the narrow end. Sew up at the bottom and if necessary at the ends using a leatherwork needle. Tie off about one third to make the head. Now clip the sheep to give it a good shape. Make ears of soft leather or felt and sew them on.

Ox and ass (Figure 4.96). Turn in the ends of a little skein of carded unspun wool. From this shape a lying ass with a few loose stitches and a fine thread. Make the ears by gently pulling out the wool. For the ox, camel hair or light brown teased sheep's wool is ideal.

The *stable* can be built of pieces of bark and twigs nailed or stuck together. Use single large pieces of bark for the roof. The stable can then be furnished with straw, moss, plants, stones and so on.

4.96 Ox and ass

Pipe-cleaner sheep

Materials

- 4 pipe-cleaners
- White unspun wool
- Darning needle
- Crochet hook No. 3 (US C/2 or D/3)
- Old scissors or pliers
- Glue

1. For the head of the sheep bend the end of a pipe-cleaner round two fingers and twist it round the neck (Figure 4.97). Make a kink for the neck.

For the forelegs bend a pipe-cleaner round the body; and do the same for the hind legs. Cut the feet to shape only when the sheep is completely finished.

2. Use the fourth pipe-cleaner to give the frame more stability and to lengthen the tail. Bend the end of the first pipe-cleaner to the front and twist it round the body.

3. Tease a bit of wool out and begin working it round the sheep at the stomach. After each turn let go of the tuft to avoid getting it twisted. Continue working round the sheep evenly from the body to the head and back again to the hind parts until it is thick enough.

Keep winding the wool to the last fibre; this will prevent it from unravelling. Do not work to the very end of the nose, or the wool will slip off.

Work the shoulders and the hind legs as follows: hold one end of the piece of wool tightly on to the left shoulder, take the wool down behind the left fore leg and back up obliquely over the chest, over the neck, crosswise over the breast to the right foreleg, back behind it and so on. In this way you form a figure of eight. Do not work the wool too tightly and make sure that it lies flat on the back. Work the hindquarters in the same way. Do not make the head too thick.

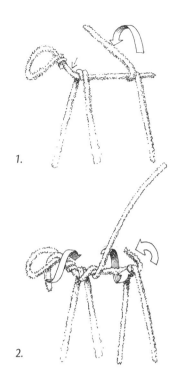

1.

2.

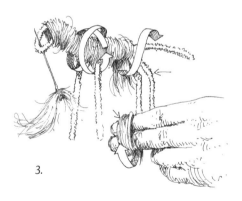

3.

4.

4.97 Making a pipe-cleaner sheep

The *nose:* Thread a bit of wool through the darning needle and secure the nose. Cover the front part also with wool.

The *tail:* Push the wool towards the hindquarters so that the tail pipe-cleaner stands free. Wind a tuft of wool over half of the pipe-cleaner. Bend the pipe-cleaner back halfway, so that the end of the tail is covered with wool. The tail should now be 2.5 cm (1 in) long. Finish off the bent-back tail with another tuft of wool, giving the tail a nice shape.

The *legs:* Push the wool of the body up a bit and wind good thin tufts of wool round the legs about halfway down. Put some glue on the lower half of the legs and continue to wind on wool. Allow the glue to dry properly and finish off by cutting the legs to the right size.

4. The *ears:* Wind a bit of wool evenly round two fingers and remove. Thrust the crochet hook carefully through the head where shown in Figure 4.97. Catch the wool in the hook and, pressing your fingers on the other side of the head, pull the hook through.

Take both ears between your thumb and forefinger and rub them into shape. Let the ears hang and fasten them with needle and thread.

You can make an *ox* and *ass* in the same way, following the pipe-cleaner shape shown in Figure 4.96.

4.98 A pipe-cleaner sheep

Geometric decorations

Three-dimensional foil shapes

Materials

- Gold foil
- Sharp scissors or a sharp knife
- Sharp pencil
- Glue
- Ruler

4.99 Tetrahedron and cube

Tetrahedron and cube

A tetrahedron is a regular solid figure contained by four regular (equilateral) triangles (Figure 4.99). Enlarge the pattern of Figure 4.100 to double its size. It is easiest to photocopy the pattern or construct it on a loose sheet of paper. This avoids unnecessary lines and marks appearing on the foil.

Lay the sheet of paper with the copied pattern on the back of the gold foil, and stick it on with two bits of adhesive tape so that it will not slip. Then draw the whole shape on to the foil.

Remove the paper and cut the shape out of the foil. To get good sharp creases fold and unfold the crease a few times before sticking down.

Spread the glue thinly on both surfaces to be stuck. Wait until the glue is nearly dry and then stick the tetrahedron together, sticking a suspension thread to the inside before closing it. Tie a few knots at the bottom of the thread so that it will not slip out of the tetrahedron. Make sure that the corners join together as exactly as possible because the glued parts are not easy to unstick.

A cube consists of six squares. The pattern in Figure 4.101 is half size. Stick the cube together in the same way as the tetrahedron.

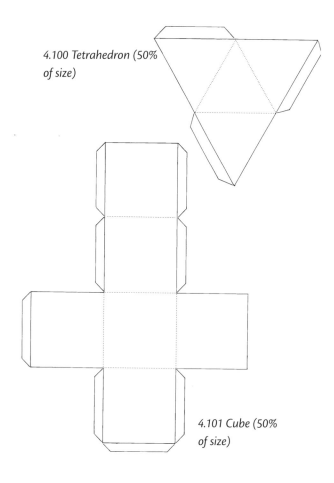

4.100 Tetrahedron (50% of size)

4.101 Cube (50% of size)

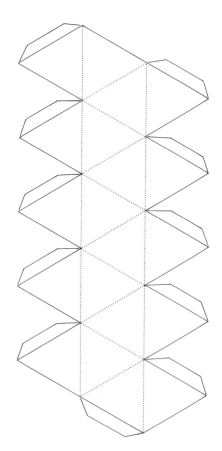

4.103 Icosahedron (60% of size)

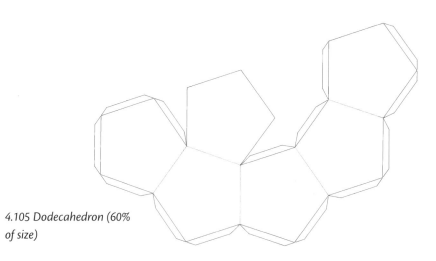

4.105 Dodecahedron (60% of size)

4.102 *Icosahedron*

4.104 *Dodecahedron*

Icosahedron

The icosahedron consists of twenty equilateral triangles (Figure 4.102). In Figure 4.103 the pattern is shown unfolded at 60% of true size.

The construction of the icosahedron is as for the tetrahedron (page 163).

Fold all the lines before beginning to glue the model, as this is no longer possible afterwards.

Leave one of the triangles open to the end, so that you can even out any irregularities from the inside using a pencil.

Dodecahedron

This shape consists of twelve regular pentagons (Figure 4.104). Figure 4.105 shows a pattern at 60% of true size for six pentagons, which make up half of the dodecahedron.

When the six pentagons are stuck together they make a bowl. Two such bowls fit exactly together (Figure 4.33, page 132), but in this model only the lower bowl needs flaps, not both bowls.

Stick the bottom half together completely, and when sticking the top half together, leave the 'lid' open.

If necessary the sticking edges can be pressed with a pencil from the inside and any irregularities removed. Before folding down the lid stick a thread to the inside of one of the corners.

4.106 Star

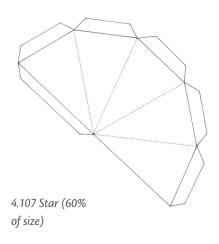

4.107 Star (60%
of size)

Star

A three-dimensional star can be made using a dodecahedron as a base (Figure 4.106).

Make twelve pentagonal pyramids, the base of each being the same size as that of the dodecahedron (Figure 4.107), and stick one pyramid on to each pentagon of the dodecahedron.

In the same way a three-dimensional star can be made from an icosahedron, in this case use twenty three-sided pyramids.

Three-dimensional straw shapes

Materials

- Straw
- Metal ruler
- Sharp knife
- Adhesive tape
- Glue
- Strong paper
- Scissors
- Thread

4.108 Straw dodecahedrons

Dodecahedrons

This dodecahedron consists of twelve regular 5-pointed stars (Figure 4.108). As a guide to determining the size of this decoration: the *side* of a pentagon is 3 cm (1¼ in); the *diagonal* of a 5-pointed star is 5 cm (2 in); the *diameter* of the whole dodecahedron will be about 8 cm (3¼ in).

Use flat ironed straw (see Straw stars on page 141). Cut the straw into thin strips with the help of a sharp knife and a metal ruler.

For a dodecahedron sixty (12 × 5) strips are needed. So calculate how many strips you can get out of one straw to avoid waste.

For this three-dimensional form it is very important that the 5-pointed stars are exactly the same size. A handy way of making the strips all the same size is to mark off the desired length on some drawing paper. Lay all the strips on the paper between the marks. Stick the straws together with some adhesive tape. Clip them to size with a pair of scissors along the marks.

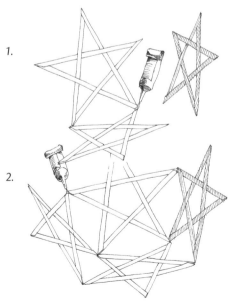

1.

2.

4.109 Making a straw dodecahedron

Construct a 5-pointed star of the desired size on a piece of paper, using Figure 4.30, page 130. Use this as a template for sticking the star together.

Take five strips and lay them with the shiny side down. Do this for each 5-pointed star.

Following the diagram in Figure 4.109, apply a little glue to the ends of two strips, one on the shiny side, one on the dull side (use a tube with a very fine nozzle, for example model-building glue). Allow the glue to dry a bit and then stick the end of the other straw on to it firmly. When interwoven as shown the five strips make a 5-pointed star. To add the third straw, apply glue to one of the ends of the two straws that are stuck together, allow it to dry a bit and stick on the third straw. In the same way stick on the last two strips.

Quickly check that the star is regular by laying it on the pattern (Figure 4.30). If necessary adjust the points before the glue sets. Make all the stars in this way and allow them to set.

Now join the stars together to form a dodecahedron by applying a little glue to all five points of the first three stars. Allow the glue to dry a bit.

1. Stick two stars together at two points (Figure 4.109, step 1). Place one of these stars on a block of wood as a base and ease the other star up so that the third star can be joined to the pair.

Apply glue to the points of the next three stars and allow to dry.

2. Stick these stars to the free points of the three stars already joined. Now half of the dodecahedron is finished.

Proceed in the same way until the whole star is finished. When you are sticking on the last star use a little more glue on one of the points so that you can attach a gold suspension thread.

Figure 4.110 shows how to make each side of the dodecahedron a pentagon with a 5-pointed star inside it. Stick all the stars together as described above, then add the links between the star-points which make up the pentagon.

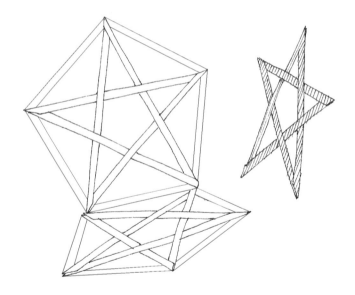

4.110 Making a straw dodecahedron

Figure 4.111 shows a smaller dodecahedron inside a larger one. For this, two complete dodecahedrons are needed, the smaller being less than two thirds of the larger.

Paint the smaller dodecahedron with a little red varnish to make it more visible or use darker straw for the smaller star.

Place the smaller dodecahedron inside the larger one before the last two stars are stuck together. Add a thread joining the smaller dodecahedron to the larger one, ensuring that the distance between them is correct.

Straw ball

Iron the straw flat (see page 141) and cut it into strips about 3 mm (1/8 in) wide. The ball in Figure 4.112 consists of eight rings.

1. Because the rings are all stuck over each other the diameter of the innermost ring must be a fraction smaller than that of the next one and so on. As the difference is scarcely perceptible the best way is to stick the two ends of the innermost ring with slightly more overlap than those of the next (Figure 4.113).

2. Make the first two rings, allow them to dry fully and then stick them together in the form of a cross, making sure that the joints of the ring don't coincide exactly. The glue of these rings stuck together must now dry fully because this is the foundation for the rest.

3. Make the remaining six rings and allow them to dry too. Then fill up the gaps between the cross in the following way: begin by sticking two rings in the middle between the cross.

4. Once this is dry stick the remaining four rings in the intervening spaces.

4.111 Small dodecahedron inside larger dodecahedron

4.112 Straw ball

Allow the glue to dry properly, then glue a piece of thread on to one of the rings. The positioning of the thread produces different effects: if it placed as in Figure 4.112 it produces the greatest effect of depth; if attached to the cross-points of the rings the ball has vertical stripes; when attached halfway between cross-points the ball has horizontal stripes. Several identical balls can create the impression that they are all different.

An extra ring placed at right angles round the other rings can be the beginning of a whole series of variations. The breadth of the rings can also be varied; indeed you can place rings touching each other all the way round so that a true ball is formed.

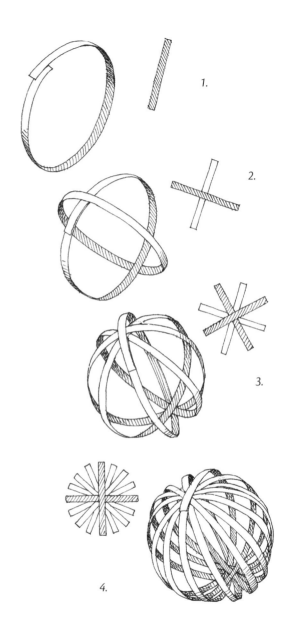

4.113 Making a straw ball

Further reading

(all Floris Books unless otherwise stated)

Adolphi, Sybille, *Making Fairy Tale Scenes*

Aeppli, Willi, *Care and Development of the Human Senses*

Anschütz, Marieke, *Children and their Temperaments*

Berger, Petra, *Feltcraft*

Berger, Thomas & Petra, *The Gnome Craft Book*

Crossley, Diana, *Muddles, Puddles and Sunshine*, Hawthorn Press

Dancy, Rahima Baldwin, *You are your Child's First Teacher*, Celestial Arts

Evans, Russell, *Helping Children to Overcome Fear*, Hawthorn Press

Fischer, Ute, *Weaving With Children*

Grunditz, Anette, *Woodworking with Children*

Guéret, Frédérique, *Magical Window Stars*

Haan, Marja de, *Knit Together, Share Together*

Hörnecke, Alice, *Paperfolding with Children*

Jaffke, Freya, *Celebrating Festivals with Children*

—, *Work and Play in Early Childhood*

Jenkinson, Sally, *The Genius of Play*, Hawthorn Press

Kaufmann, Birte, *Gardening Classes in Waldorf Schools*

König, Karl, *The First Three Years of the Child*

Kornberger, Horst, *The Power of Stories*

Kronshage, Michaela, *Transparent Window Scenes Through the Year*

Kutsch, Irmgard and Brigitte Walden, *Spring and Summer Nature Activities for Waldorf Kindergartens*

—, *Autumn and Winter Nature Activities for Waldorf Kindergartens*

Leeuwen, M van & J Moeskops, *The Nature Corner*

Mellon, Nancy, *Storytelling with Children*, Hawthorn Press

Meyer, Rudolf, *The Wisdom of Fairy Tales*

Müller, Brunhild, *Painting with Children*

Neuschütz, Karin, *Sewing Dolls*

—, *Making Soft Toys*

—, *Creative Wool: Making Woollen Crafts with Children*

Oldfield, Lynne, *Free to Learn*, Hawthorn Press

Petrash, Carol, *Earthwise: Environmental Crafts and Activities with Young Children*

Rawson, Martyn & Michael Rose, *Ready to Learn*, Hawthorn Press

Reinhard, Rotraud, *Crafting a Felt Farm*

—, *Magic Natural Felt Animals*

Schäfer, Christine, *Magic Wool Fruit Children*

—, *Magic Wool Fairies*

—, *Magic Wool Mermaids and Fairies*

Taylor, Michael, *Finger Strings*

Ulke, Viola, *Making a Nativity Scene*

Wendt, Caroline & Pernilla Wästberg, *A Swedish Christmas*

Wolk-Gerche, Angelika, *Crocheting Soft Toys*

—, *More Magic Wool*

—, *Papercraft*

Resources

Recommended sources for magic
wool and natural materials:

AUSTRALIA
Morning Star
www.morningstarcrafts.com.au

Winterwood Toys
www.winterwoodtoys.com.au

NORTH AMERICA
Bella Luna Toys
www.bellalunatoys.com

A Child's Dream
www.achildsdream.com

The Waldorf Shop
www.waldorfshop.net

UK
Conscious Craft
www.consciouscraft.co.uk

Myriad Natural Toys
www.myriadonline.co.uk

A selection of craft and activity books for children and adults

Magic Wool Fairies
How to make seasonal fairies and angels
Christine Schäfer

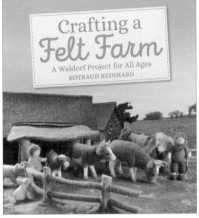

Crafting a **Felt Farm**
A Waldorf Project for All Ages
ROTRAUD REINHARD

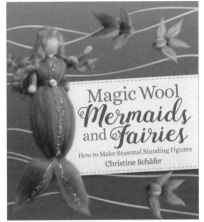

Magic Wool Mermaids and Fairies
How to Make Seasonal Standing Figures
Christine Schäfer

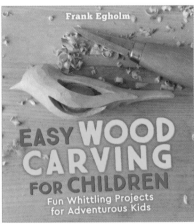

Frank Egholm

EASY WOOD CARVING FOR CHILDREN
Fun Whittling Projects for Adventurous Kids

Transparent Window Scenes Through the Year
Michaela Kronshage and Sylvia Schwartz

The Nature Corner
Celebrating the year's cycle with seasonal tableaux
M. van Leeuwen and J. Moeskops

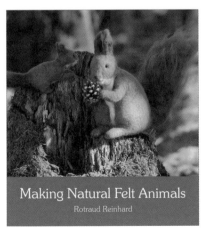

Making Natural Felt Animals
Rotraud Reinhard

Crocheting Soft Toys
Angelika Wolk-Gerche

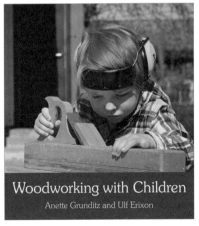

Woodworking with Children
Anette Grunditz and Ulf Erixon

Spring and Summer Nature Activities for Waldorf Kindergartens

Irmgard Kutsch · Brigitte Walden

Autumn and Winter Nature Activities for Waldorf Kindergartens

Irmgard Kutsch · Brigitte Walden

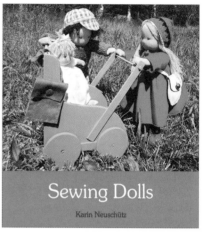

Sewing Dolls

Karin Neuschütz

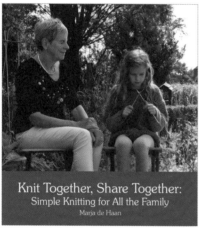

Knit Together, Share Together:
Simple Knitting for All the Family
Marja de Haan

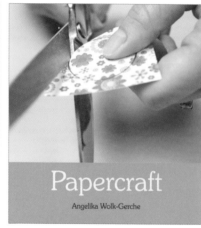

Papercraft

Angelika Wolk-Gerche

Making a Nativity Scene

Christmas Figures and Animals for a Seasonal Display

Viola Ulke

The Gnome Craft Book

Thomas and Petra Berger

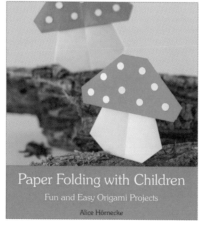

Paper Folding with Children
Fun and Easy Origami Projects
Alice Hörnecke

Feltcraft
Making Dolls, Gifts and Toys
Petra Berger

florisbooks.co.uk

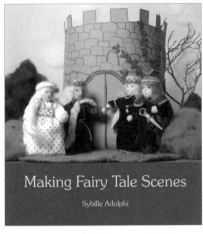

Making Fairy Tale Scenes

Sybille Adolphi

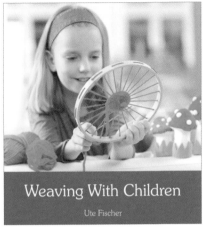

Weaving With Children

Ute Fischer

Magical Window Stars

Frédérique Guéret

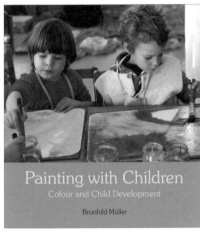

Painting with Children

Colour and Child Development

Brunhild Müller

Making Soft Toys

Karin Neuschütz

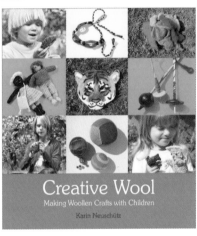

Creative Wool

Making Woollen Crafts with Children

Karin Neuschütz

A SWEDISH CHRISTMAS

Simple Scandinavian Crafts, Recipes and Decorations

CAROLINE WENDT AND PERNILLA WÄSTBERG

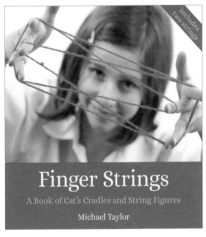

includes two strings

Finger Strings

A Book of Cat's Cradles and String Figures

Michael Taylor

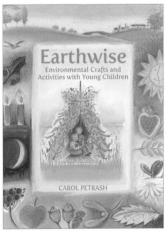

Earthwise

Environmental Crafts and Activities with Young Children

CAROL PETRASH

Floris
Books